WHITEMAN'S
GOSPEL

"Craig Smith issues a call from the wilderness, the wilderness of Native America. The call for recognition, respect and responsibility. First of all, it is a call for recognition of the Native church that has often been marginalized by paternalistic religious authorities. Second, it is a call to respect for Native American people and their cultures. I am most encouraged by Craig's call for Native Christians to decide how Christianity should relate to and judge their culture. Third, this book is a call to responsibility for Native American Christians for their culture, their churches, their morality, and their future. I hope Christian America responds with acknowledgment and tangible respect. I hope we, as Native people, rise to the challenge and make a difference!"

Adrian Jacobs, Executive Director
First Nations Centre for Ministry,
Belleville, Ontario

"WHITE MAN'S GOSPEL is a "must read" for anyone interested in the progress of the gospel among America's First Peoples. After more than five hundred years, Christian churches are still searching for the key to the hearts of Native American people. This book explores the reasons why. As a Native American and an evangelist, Craig Smith writes from the perspective of an insider. His experience as a denominational administrator and a church planter provides him with unique insight into the reasons why Native people continue to resist the message of the cross. Not everyone will like what they read here. The book is sure to stir controversy. However, regardless of whether or not you choose to agree with him, Smith raises issues that deserve to be given careful attention."

Rev. Daniel R. Wetzel
District Superintendent Southwestern District
The Christian and Missionary Alliance

"Some books are groundbreaking classics in their content. This is one of them. It challenges, it provokes and gives wisdom. I was personally humbled and refreshed as I read the manuscript. This book is a must for anyone interested in working with our Aboriginal people."

Rev. Dietrich Desmarais
Bethlehem Aboriginal Fellowship
Winnipeg, Manitoba

WHITEMAN'S
GOSPEL

A Native American
examines the
Christian Church and its
ministry among
Native Americans

CRAIG STEPHEN SMITH

INDIAN LIFE BOOKS

Published by Indian Life Books

A Division of Intertribal Christian Communications
P.O. Box 3765, Redwood Postal Outlet
Winnipeg, Manitoba R2W 3R6

ISBN 0-920379-12-5

First published 1997, Second printing 1998, Third printing 2001,
Fourth printing 2006, Fifth printing 2010, Sixth printing 2014

Unless otherwise marked, all Scripture quotations are from *Holy Bible,
New International Version (NIV)*, published by Zondervan Bible Publishers, Copyright © International Bible Society. Used by permission.

The publishers wish to thank the following publishers for permission to
quote from their publications: Simon & Schuster, publishers of
CUSTER DIED FOR YOUR SINS: AN INDIAN MANIFESTO by
Vine Deloria, Jr., Copyright © Vine Deloria, Jr., Alfred A. Knopf,
publishers of NOW THAT THE BUFFALO'S GONE by Alvin M.
Josephy, Jr., Copyright © Alvin M. Josephy, Jr.

Printed and bound in Canada.

Visit Indian Life Ministries' web site at www.indianlife.org

Author's note:
The terms "Native," "Indian," and "Native American" are used interchange-
ably throughout the book. Also, the term Native American Church and Native Church are used. The Native American Church refers specifically to the
Peyote Movement, while Native Church refers to the Native Christian Church.

DEDICATION

To LaDonna,
my wife and best friend

TABLE OF CONTENTS

FOREWORD

THEN YOU WILL KNOW the truth, and the truth will set you free!

This is one book that should be read by every man and woman in North America.

My brother and friend Craig Smith, a Chippewa, is offering the Church of Jesus Christ some truths that I believe have the potential to break down walls. These thick walls have been dividing the Native peoples of our land from those of us whose descendants come from Europe—walls of ignorance and stereotypes—walls of injustices and racism and walls of condescension mistakenly intended as ministry.

But Craig does more than point a finger at the walls, he describes the bridge that Jesus Christ built when He lived among us as a member of a tribe and a minority group colonized by the dominant society of the day—the Romans. Craig describes God's fingerprints in Native Culture and offers a pathway of hope and healing for all of us, Native or non-Native.

As you read this book, you will read the truth about Native culture and Native pain. May the truth break down the walls in your heart with a fresh view of how Jesus Christ came to heal and forgive.

It is the truth that will set you free! And you will be free indeed!

Bill McCartney, *Founder of Promise Keepers*

PREFACE

THE ABORIGINAL PEOPLE of North America are one
of the most resistant people groups to the Gospel of Jesus Christ
in the world today. That resistance has developed over the years
and is due to a variety of reasons. Some of this resistance is
self-imposed. There is also a history of mistakes, mismanage-
ment, and counter-productive methodologies on the part of the
Body of Christ.

For centuries the saving message of the Gospel of Jesus Christ
has been presented here in North America to the original inhabitants of this land, often with very little results. Gospel ministry
in aboriginal North America today is often times very difficult
and slow, and the purveyors of contemporary Christianity often
find themselves among a resistant and hardened people.

I know. Not only am I a minister of the Gospel of Jesus
Christ, but I am a North American aboriginal person. All my
life I have had the opportunity to witness personally this pain-
fully slow process of winning Indian people to Christ, and, from
a ministry perspective that spans over a quarter century, I've
seen the Body of Christ struggle to find the most appropriate
methodology that would meet the needs of this unique segment
of North American society.

I have lived in both worlds (Indian and white). It's been equally
frustrating, as a minister, to deal with the way Native people
reject the gospel without giving it a fair hearing. As a Native
person, I've also been frustrated by the way the Church continues in its oft-times counter-productive ways to minister only
producing little or no results.

The idea for this book was born in my heart about ten years

ago, as I was assuming the mantle of Native leadership within my denomination's ministry. As I began to write down the ideas and thoughts about Native ministry, I began to realize that I was living in a high level of frustration, which was, at times, all-consuming in my life. I was frustrated at my people for the hardness of heart to the gospel that really didn't need to be there if they only had a true understanding of what the gospel really is all about. I was equally disheartened with the Church for what I saw was a multitude of wrongful acts, done to the Native North American people in the past and even today in the name of Christ.

My personality is that of a sanguine. A sanguine is a happy-go-lucky person, with no real worries, who looks at life usually from a positive perspective. So for me to be brought to a level of intense frustration, anger and anxiety was very much out of context with who I really was.

It has taken me several years to work through that frustration, and I now feel that the Lord has brought me through the fire. The Lord has been impressing on me the need to put these thoughts down on paper, and I sense that now is the time to write, not out of frustration, but as a soldier who was wounded and is now well on the way to being healed.

That allows me, hopefully, to write from the kind of perspective that is needed to bring about positive change. It is from that perspective that I share what I hope will be helpful observations and practical solutions to the questions many are asking regarding ministry to Native Americans.

My experiences have led me to believe that change is desperately needed in both the Native and ecclesiastical communities. We also need to look back historically to see where the root of the problem lies. The history of Indian and white relations and the Church's involvement with our people led me to one difficult conclusion.

Jesus Christ said, "I will build My church." Those whom He has commissioned to carry out His command have yet to fulfill the mandate to reach Native North Americans effectively, and in a way that is culturally sensitive and allows the gospel to deal with our people in light of their cultures. We aren't there yet, and in some ways, we have a long way to go.

But we as Native Americans also need to look at ourselves, and see where we have been wrong in our perceptions of Christianity. Native people have often hidden behind the notion that the gospel is the "White Man's Gospel," without really knowing what they are speaking about.

One of our Native pastors made an interesting observation recently. He said, "Christianity has wonderful answers to questions Indians aren't asking!"

That statement was made during a meeting of Christian Indian leaders struggling with the issues of Christianity and Native culture. We were trying to discuss the issue of perceived irrelevancy of the gospel in the minds of many Native Americans today.

That statement has stayed with me to this day, and has caused me to attempt to evaluate why many Native people think this way.

I do agree with this pastor's observation, and I think it goes to the heart of what I feel are major changes that need to be made in our thinking in both the Indian community and within the Body of Christ.

I would desire, through this book, to turn the light of illumination on within these two communities, so that we can see each other more appropriately and more accurately, and understand each other's true hearts.

It is my desire to build bridges, not walls, through the issues I raise. Once those bridges are established, both communities need to be willing to cross over to the other side, and begin the process of healing and reconciling in the past, making right the present, and planning for better days in the future.

I share these thoughts with you with the desire and prayer that the glorious Gospel of Jesus Christ will be given a fair hearing by my people, and that the Body of Christ will be relevant enough in its methodologies to provide a climate for that to happen.

To that end, I am committed.

Craig Stephen Smith
White Earth Band of Chippewa Indians

ACKNOWLEDGEMENTS

I AM GRATEFUL to all those who provided the motivation and encouragement to embark on this new experience—writing a book. I have had these thoughts in my mind for many years, but it took some wonderful people who believed in me and my thoughts, to move those thoughts from my mind to the finished book in front of you.

I first must give credit to my wife, LaDonna, without whom my life would not be complete. She has been with me through the good and bad experiences of my life, and has always remained a steady source of godliness and love. She has provided the greatest source of encouragement and support for this project. Without her, I could not have done it!

I also want to thank Coach Bill McCartney, founder of Promise Keepers, who, in June 1995, during a meeting between minority clergy leaders and the Promise Keepers organizational leadership, encouraged me to write. This came at a time when I was petitioning the Lord in this regard. I also want to thank my good friend Matthew Parker for his encouragement and mentorship through this process.

This book would not be complete without the help of some key friends and ministry colleagues who generously gave of their time and thoughts in reviewing the original manuscript, which has gone through much revision and editing. My thanks go to Dr. Keith M. Bailey, Dr. John L. Ng, Rev. Herman J. Williams, Rev. Randy Phillips, Rev. Tom Claus, Dr. Emerson Falls, Rev. Huron Claus, Dr. Russell Begaye and Rev. L.W. (Bud) Elford, for all their wisdom and input.

Brothers, my heart's desire and prayer to God for the Israelites is that they may be saved. For I can testify about them that they are zealous for God, but their zeal is not based upon knowledge. Since they did not know the righteousness that comes from God and sought to establish their own, they did not submit to God's righteousness. Christ is the end of the law so that there may be righteousness for everyone who believes.

—Romans 10:1-4

Chapter 1

The Bible
and the
Whiteman's Gospel

"JESUS CHRIST IS A WHITE MAN!" The words of that
Native man ring in my ears today as clear as if 1973 were yesterday.
"Jesus Christ is a white man! I cannot accept a Savior who is a
white man! We must all reject this White Man's Gospel!"

There are certain experiences in a person's life that even the
most minor details of that experience remain vivid in their
memory, though the event occurred perhaps years ago.

Such is the case for me as I recall those stinging words as I
was sitting on the top row of the bleachers in my high school
gymnasium one afternoon.

The high school principal's militaristic voice rang loud and
clear over the school's intercom system.

"All Indian students are to be excused from class and are to
assemble on the bleachers of the gym immediately."

For me, any reason to get out of class was reason enough to
rejoice, and I can recall joking and laughing with other students
coming out of classrooms as we made our way to the gym.

"Well, at least now we can finally say that there are some
advantages to being an Indian," a friend said as we got to the
gym.

"Wonder what's going on in the gym?" another said inquisitively.

I remember going into the gym, climbing to the top of the bleachers, and feeling the cold of the cement block wall making its way through my back and into my body. The chill of that wall was nothing in comparison to the chill that I would experience over the next forty-five minutes as the surprise assembly convened.

As the principal approached the microphone, you could tell there was an obvious look of concern on his face as he began to bring the gathering to order. He stammered and hunted for words and seemed to make more of a fool of himself than what we as students usually gave him credit for.

That look of concern on his face was not anything new in Cass Lake, especially during those tumultuous days of 1973.

What had been a fairly normal, small, quiet town in northern Minnesota had become a hotbed of racial tension and turmoil as of late.

Only a few short months prior, in an area far removed from our town, a major turning point in Indian affairs and relations had occurred—the standoff at Wounded Knee, South Dakota.

The growing animosity between Indians and the U.S. government reached a boiling point there, and in the wake of that occupation and confrontation, lives were lost. A new era of Indian identity and militancy emerged, led by the "Red Power" movement.

To some, the events in South Dakota seemed to be an isolated incident, but the ripple effects of that encounter were spreading all throughout Indian country, including our area.

The sleepy little town of Cass Lake, Minnesota was also experiencing a turmoil of its own during those days. Tension was building between the Indians and the whites, and nobody knew where it would lead.

Cass Lake was a town that literally was divided down the middle by what used to be the railroad tracks my father and his brother and sister used to play around. After the railroad tracks were moved and U.S. Highway 2 was installed in its place, it still provided the defining line between the two cultures in our town.

North of Highway 2 was Tract 33, Indian land, and home to all the tribal offices and agencies. South of Highway 2 was where the privately owned land was, where most of the white folk lived. There were some Indian families that lived on the south side of the highway, including, incidentally, our family as I was growing up.

I don't actually recall how the tension began to build in the early 1970s, but tension there was. The tribal leadership had erected a huge billboard on the north side of Highway 2, facing across the highway to the "other side of the tracks." That billboard resembled a huge marquee where messages from the tribal leadership could be displayed. Sometimes hostile messages were displayed against prominent and not so prominent members of the non-Indian community, and the tension was close to reaching the boiling point between the two cultures.

Shortly after Wounded Knee, a militant Indian faction was planning on making their presence known in Cass Lake by holding a gathering there.

Fears of outright violence gripped the community, and thoughts of another Wounded Knee abounded. Many non-Indian people were planning to board up their homes and leave until things settled down.

In the midst of all this tension in our community, there I sat, on the top row of the bleachers listening to my principal introduce an Indian man who was to speak to us as Indian students.

I don't recall his name, nor do I recall his tribal affiliation, although I believe he was Lakota. He began by telling us some background information about himself, and then he proceeded to impress upon us the need for Indian people to begin rising up and recapturing the identity that centuries of contact with the white man had been taken away from us piece by piece.

After what seemed to be about a forty-five minute lecture, he was bringing to a close his powerfully moving speech.

As he was about ready to close, he said he had one more

thing to say to us.

He told us that if we are going to be successful in recapturing and retaining our identity as Indian nations, then we all must rise up and reject what he called "The Whiteman's Gospel" and return to the gods of our ancestors.

He had concluded that the message of Jesus Christ was not a message that we can accept if we are going to be a real Indian. In fact, I can still remember to this day those actual words that cut through me like a knife. He angrily stated, "Jesus Christ is a white man! Jesus Christ is a white man! I cannot accept a Savior who is a white man! We all must reject this Whiteman's Gospel!"

I recall sitting there, stunned, as many friends of mine gathered around this man, shaking his hand, patting him on the back, and treating him with almost celebrity status. I felt like someone had just stuck a knife through my spiritual heart, and I knew for the first time in my life what that old saying, "my heart bled," must have meant.

You see, it had not yet been two years since I had surrendered my life to Jesus Christ, and though I was raised in an Indian Christian home, my own spiritual growth was only in the infancy stage. Now, the whole basis for the life I was living was being challenged, and I felt I was the only one in that cavernous gymnasium who had, as it were, his spiritual life crucified on an altar of Indian identity.

"Jesus Christ is a white man!"

Unfortunately, that wasn't the last time I was to hear those words, and hear Indian people say that Christianity is the "Whiteman's Gospel."

In the years to follow, as I have been walking with Jesus and ministering among my people, often have been the times Indian people have told me that they don't want to hear about Christ, because He's the white man's God, and it's the Whiteman's Gospel.

For so many Indian people, this has become the buzz word and phrase to excuse themselves from giving any serious thought to the claims of Jesus Christ.

I feel like I can relate to the apostle Paul as he wrote to the Romans the Scripture passage at the beginning of this chapter.

He says that his prayer to God for his people is that they would be saved. Well, that's my prayer as well for my people, that ultimately, they would be saved.

He gives his people credit, as I give my people credit, that they have a tremendous zeal for God. You can't participate in the traditional ceremonies such as the Plains Indian Sun dance, where they pierce their flesh and are attached by rope to that tall pole and pull away until their flesh tears, without zeal.

But Paul says that Israel's zeal is not based on knowledge.

I believe so strongly that the main thing keeping Native North Americans away from the reality of the gospel is knowledge. Knowledge of what the gospel is really about, and knowledge that will dispel the notion that the gospel is the "Whiteman's Gospel." For many of my people, the methods that were used historically overshadowed and nullified the message of Christ, so that many won't give consideration to the wonderful saving message of Christ and Calvary.

I believe it is incumbent on us as Native Christians to help our people understand that the message of Jesus Christ is not the "Whiteman's Gospel," but is our Creator's plan for the redemption of all mankind, including the Native North Americans.

We must address head on the mistakes of the past, and offer positive solutions on dealing with them. When the church really sees what it has done in the past, the natural response will be to repent and seek biblical reconciliation with Native North Americans.

Increasing the knowledge of salvation, focusing on the message, and not the methods that have been so damaging in reaching our people must be what we are about today in Native work. If we will do that, we will provide one of the most important services to our people, that will help change their eternal destiny.

How do we present the knowledge of salvation to this distinct and multi-cultural people known as Native North Americans? How do we approach Native ministry in a way that we can build disciples and have fruit that remains?

I believe the first step in effectively reaching Native Americans is to dispel the notion of the "Whiteman's Gospel." But how is that done?

It's done by giving careful thought and analysis as to why the notion of Christ being a white man and His gospel the Whiteman's Gospel is present in so many Native people's lives. In order to do this, we will need to do several things.

First, we must be willing to give credence to the writings of Holy Scripture, the Bible. That shouldn't be too difficult for the majority of open-minded Indian people, for even some of the modern day Indian spirituality movements incorporate the Bible in their proceedings. Some in the Native American Church, or Peyote movement, will incorporate the reading of Scripture, and many of the wise elders of our nations affirm the wisdom contained in its teachings.

We need to start with the basic teachings found in the pages of the Bible. What do these truths say to us as Native people, and how do we apply its message?

A Basic Biblical Overview

The basic foundational teachings of Christianity, clearly illustrated for us throughout the whole of the Bible, center around the following truths:

First, there is a triune God, comprising of God the Father, God the Son, and God the Holy Spirit (just as we are triune beings, complete with a body, soul and spirit). This triune God is the Supreme Being, and He is the Creator of the universe. In the process of creation, He made man the highest level of creation. Recognizing man's need for a helpmate, he took from man a rib and created woman. Together they were to be united as the capstone of all God's creation.

The first man and woman, Adam and Eve, were tempted in the garden by the serpent who caused them to disobey God their Creator, by eating the forbidden fruit. From that moment, the earth was cursed with sin, because of their disobedience, and all of mankind, including every race has been under sin's curse, resulting in death and separation from God.

As the earth was populated, God began the process of redeeming back His highest creation, so that He could be worshipped and adored by His creation.

The Bible teaches that God is a just and righteous God and must punish sin. If He didn't, He wouldn't be just and holy. As much as God hates sin, He loves the sinner, and went to the ultimate extreme to pay the penalty for man's sin.

He sent His only Son, Jesus Christ, to earth, to live a sinless life, and to pay the ultimate price, the shedding of His blood, for the remission of sins. Jesus was crucified, buried, and rose again on the third day, and shortly afterwards, He ascended back to heaven where He is now seated at the right hand of the Father, interceding for those who trust in Him.

The Bible gives us the assurance that at this time, Jesus is preparing heaven to be occupied by those who have accepted Him as their Savior. Heaven is a reality for the Christian, because the Bible tells us that God will ultimately, once and for all deal with the curse of sin by destroying the earth as we know it, and all who reject His plan of salvation.

We are living today in a time of grace, where God is allowing His creation opportunity to escape the wrath to come, which will be poured out in the last days.

Salvation comes to an individual by confessing their sins to God, and believing that Jesus Christ paid the penalty for their sins on the cross, and trusting completely in what He did on the cross for the payment of the penalty of our sin.

By accepting this free gift of salvation, we are assured of escape from eternal separation from God, and we become His children.

He has given to those who accept Christ's substitutionary death the power of the indwelling Spirit of God to live victorious lives here on earth, and to protect the Christian from the powers of the enemy of our soul, Satan, himself.

That is the basic, foundational teaching of the Bible.

But let me ask, what does the Bible say about this central figure of the Bible, the man, Jesus Christ? Is it appropriate for

Indian people to call him a white man?

The miracle of the Son of God coming down to earth, taking on the form of man, and living among His creation is intriguing, to say the least.

Since God was going to do this, what were the details that He had to work out in order to make it happen?

Since God is God, He is all powerful and can do anything He wants. The ability He has to allow Himself to be made manifest as a human being is unquestionable. He could do it without any problem.

The Lord was ultimately interested in the details of how the incarnate Christ would be revealed to the world. After all, it was God who instituted the different people groups of the world when He confused the languages at the Tower of Babel centuries before. If He was to come to earth as a man, what people group would He come through? Or, would He be this generic Person with no identity to any particular people group?

God was committed to identify Himself through the incarnate Christ with one of the nations of the earth. The question is, what nation would He choose, and what would be the rationale for His choice?

This question is of ultimate importance to Indian people as we seek the truth of many Indians' claim that Jesus was a white man, and that the gospel is the "Whiteman's Gospel."

Not only is the Bible the inspired Word of God, it provides us with an abundance of history that is presented without bias and is completely trustworthy. Unlike the many tainted and biased history books written about American and Canadian history and how our people are portrayed, the Bible is full of truth, not error, fact, not fiction, and reality, not illusion.

Through what people group did God reveal Himself to the world? The Bible tells us that God, in his infinite wisdom, chose one man, one individual, named Abram, to lay the generational foundation for the Savior of the world to be born through.

In the Old Testament we read about this man, Abram. In the first book of the Bible, we read the following:

The Lord had said to Abram, "Leave your country, your people, and your father's household and go to the land I will show you. I will make you into a great nation and I will bless you; I will make your name great and you will be a blessing. I will bless those who bless you, and whoever curses you I will curse; and all peoples on earth will be blessed through you." Genesis 12:1-3

Here we have the first recorded covenant God made between a select people group ever recorded in Scripture. The blessing was to be with Abram and his descendants. In fact, in chapter 17 we read:

When Abram was ninety-nine years old, the Lord appeared to him and said, "I am God Almighty, walk before me and be blameless. I will confirm my covenant with you and will greatly increase your numbers." Abram fell face down and God said to him, "As for me, this is my covenant with you: You will be the father of many nations. No longer will you be called Abram; your name will be Abraham, for I have made you a father of many nations. I will make you very fruitful; I will make nations of you, and kings will come from you. I will establish my covenant as an everlasting covenant between me and you and your descendants after you for the generations to come, to be your God and the God of your descendants after you..."
Genesis 17:1-7

The covenant God made between Abraham and Himself was an amazing covenant, especially because Abraham's wife, Sarah was barren. Abraham had already slept with Sarah's maid servant, Hagar, and she bore him a son named Ishmael. But the covenant was not to be with Ishmael and his descendants, but with another son that Abraham and Sarah, though now past child-bearing years, would have.

God told Abraham he would have a son and he would be called Isaac. When Sarah conceived and bore Isaac, there was great rejoicing. What about Hagar and Ishmael, though? Sarah had sent them away, and they fled for their lives. The Bible says that an angel of the Lord found her, pregnant with Ishmael, wandering in the wilderness. The angel of the Lord prophesied over Hagar, regarding her son, soon to be born. This is what the angel said about Ishmael, and his descendants:

You are now with a child and you will have a son. You will name him Ishmael, for the Lord has heard your misery. He will be a wild donkey of a man; his hand will be against everyone and everyone's hand against him, and he will live in hostility toward all his brothers.
Genesis 16:11-12

Who became the descendants of Ishmael, whose father was Abraham and mother was Hagar? His descendants are the Arab people of the world. Isn't it interesting to see the prophecy over Ishmael and his descendants, and compare that prophecy with the history and current status of Arab peoples around the world?

There usually isn't a day that goes by where Arab and Israeli conflict is not reported on the nightly newscasts. God's Word is true!

God's covenant agreement was not with Abraham's son Ishmael, but with his other son, Isaac. But it must be clear that though this was the case, God also had a place in His creation for the Arab peoples. There is no group of people ever created that should ever be considered mistakes, or inferior to any other people. God did, however, set apart one specific people to be the ones through whom the Savior of the world would come to us. The child Isaac was to be conceived between Abraham and his real wife, Sarah. The challenge was that Sarah was barren all her life, and now both were more ready for the nursing home than a romp in the bedroom, because he was almost a hundred years old and she was already ninety!

Conceive, she did, and they called their son Isaac.

When Isaac grew up, he married Rebekah, and they had twin sons, Jacob and Esau. Even within the womb, these two brothers were jostling with each other. Rebekah went to the Lord and asked why, even in the womb, would these twins be fighting against each other.

God's reply was clear.

Two nations are in your womb, and two peoples from within you will be separated; one people will be stronger than the other, and the older will serve the younger. Genesis 25:23

When she gave birth, Esau came out first, and Jacob followed. When they had grown up, Esau was a skillful hunter, while his brother Jacob was the quiet, shy type, staying around home. Isaac, the father, had a special love for his first born, Esau, but mom loved her son Jacob.

Once, the younger Jacob was making some stew, and his older twin came in from hunting. Esau was hungry and asked Jacob for some of the stew. Jacob said he would give him some, but first he must sell him his birthright. The Bible says that Esau despised his birthright, and sold it outright to Jacob.

Not only did Jacob steal his older brother's birthright, but he also in a deceitful way stole the blessing of his dying father from Esau. This blessing was going to be given to Esau from his father, but as he was out hunting for food for the feast, Jacob tricked his father into receiving the blessing instead.

Jacob married two sisters, Leah and Rachel, and twelve sons were born to him. The original covenant that God made with Abraham passed down through his son Isaac, to his son, Jacob, whose name was later changed to Israel, and eventually to his twelve sons, the children of Israel, or the Israelites.

This somewhat involved walk back through Biblical history points to the fact that God, in His infinite wisdom and knowledge, chose the seed of Abraham, Isaac and Jacob, to be the chosen people group to not only enter into a covenant with, but eventually be the people group that the incarnate Christ would be revealed through.

What does the Bible say regarding the culture of this chosen people group, the Israelites? We go to another Old Testament book to find out what God says about this group:

> *For you are a people holy to the Lord your God. The Lord your God has chosen you out of all the peoples on the face of the earth to be his people, his treasured possession. The Lord did not set his affection on you and choose you because you were more numerous than other peoples, for you were the fewest of all peoples.*

> *Deuteronomy 7:6-7*

This is an important history lesson for Indian people, and an important truth in dispelling the notion that Jesus was a white man and his message is the Whiteman's Gospel.

The truth that must be told is this: Jesus was born into a minority group!

Not only was He born into a minority group, but according to these verses the Israelites were the fewest of the few! They were, numerically, at the bottom of the ladder.

Don't you think God could have done better than that?

Why would He, in his infinite wisdom and knowledge, choose, in the eyes of the rest of the world, the lowest of the low, fewest of the few, smallest of the small, to be the channel for bringing His incarnate Christ into the world?

But let's not stop there. You see, not only did God send His Son into the world through a minority group, He sent His Son into the world through a tribal group!

That's right! A tribal group!

Remember, we said that Israel had twelve sons? What does the Bible say about these twelve sons? Who were they?

Back in Genesis chapter 49, we read that Jacob (later known as Israel) called together his sons just before he died. His sons' names, as recorded in Genesis 49 are Reuben, Simeon, Levi, Judah, Zebulun, Issachar, Dan, Gad, Asher, Naphtali, Joseph and Benjamin.

Note with me, what Scripture says about these twelve sons:

All these are the twelve tribes of Israel, and this is what their father said to them when he blessed them, giving each the blessing appropriate to him. Genesis 49:28

From Abraham to Isaac to Jacob to Judah and eventually down to King David were fourteen generations, and from King David to the exile in Babylon was another fourteen generations, and from the exile in Babylon to the birth of Jesus Christ was another fourteen generations. A total of 42 generations and thousands of years passed from God's initial covenant with Abraham, to when Jesus Christ would be born.

He was born into the world as a descendant of Abraham, Isaac and Israel, a member of a minority group, which was the smallest, most insignificant people group on the face of the earth, which incidentally was divided into twelve tribes.

We can look to the historical facts that discount the claims of many Indian people that Jesus was a white man. We can also look to the time of Christ for further facts which shed light on the fallacy that keeps many Indian people from Christ.

Any student of history will attest to the fact that the history of the Israeli people has been anything but easy. All the way back to the slavery in Egypt, to the Canaanites, Philistines, Syrians, Assyrians, Babylonians, Romans, and even up to our recollections of Hitler's execution of more than six million Jews, to their ongoing battles with the descendants of Ishmael, the Arabs, the Jewish story is a journey through troubles, trials, and a literal fight for their own survival.

What was it like politically for the Israelites during the time of Christ?

The Bible once again gives us clear and unbiased reporting on such details as the political climate of the day, nearly two thousand years ago when Jesus walked on the earth. Should that seem to be insufficient, there are other historians, like a man named Josephus, who was not a believer in Christ, who can attest to what life was like during those days.

During that particular time in the history of the world, there was one people group that would have been given the description of "superpower." That power was the mighty Roman Empire.

The tentacles of the Roman Empire spread from Rome all throughout the then known world. The Emperor, Caesar Augustus, ruled country after country from his lofty perch in the city of Rome.

One of the countries that had been taken by the Romans was Palestine, what the Israelites called home.

During the time of Christ, the roads of Palestine were patrolled by the occupying Roman soldiers, and the political system of Rome had been established in Jerusalem with an iron fist.

In fact, in the gospel of Luke, chapter 2, we read:

In those days Caesar Augustus issued a decree that a census should be taken of the entire Roman world. (This was the first census that took place while Quirinius was governor of Syria). And everyone went to his own town to register. So Joseph also went up from the town of Nazareth in Galilee to Judea, to Bethlehem, the town of David, because he belonged to the house and line of David. Luke 2:1-4

Here is another concept, based upon historical fact, that we need to understand as we deal with the notion of the gospel being the Whiteman's Gospel.

Not only was Jesus born into a minority group, and not only was He born into a tribal group. He was born in the ancestral homeland of His people, and that land was under the rule of a dominant society, namely the Roman Empire.

That sure sounds like our people today! In fact, Jesus and His earthly family experienced some of the same kinds of atrocities, at the hands of the dominant society that our people faced.

We are all aware of the Cherokees forced march from the eastern seaboard to the plains of Oklahoma in what has been described as their "Trail of Tears." My wife's tribe, the Navajo, were also involved in a forced march, called "The Long Walk." These forced exiles from ancestral homelands of our people were some of the darkest days in the history of Native America, and they illustrate the tremendous animosity evident in the early days of Indian and White relations.

Thousands of Cherokees were forced to move from their homeland in the mountains of the eastern seaboard to the plains of Oklahoma under U.S. president Andrew Jackson's orders. Thousands of Navajos faced a similar fate as they too were exiled from their homes. To add insult to injury, the government soldiers passed out blankets laced with various types of diseases to the Navajos under the pretense of keeping them warm after their Long Walk had ended. Many who survived the tortures of the walk became even further weakened by the diseased blankets they wrapped themselves in—in order to keep warm against the cold of that dreadful winter season.

Such is the case for Jesus and His parents, Mary and Joseph, in what we affectionately refer to as the Christmas story. Their journey from Nazareth to Bethlehem was no easy task. Caesar's decree forced them to travel many miles over rough terrain, Joseph on foot, and Mary on a donkey, while Mary was close to giving birth.. It was their own Long Walk. It was their own Trail of Tears. Jesus knows what our people have gone through!

I was born in the ancestral (well, not so ancestral, since our Algonquin roots go back to the east coast and we had to battle the Sioux for the woodlands) homeland of my people, but we also were and are under the rule of a dominant society.

For the Israelites, life during the time of Christ was a mixture of their own culture, traditions, language, and customs, but they also were accountable to the Roman Empire, including taxation, and submission to Roman law.

Such is the case for us as Native people today. We live with the same mixture of traditional culture, values, traditions, languages and customs, but we also pay taxes, not to Caesar, but to Uncle Sam. We don't send it to Rome. We send it to Washington, D.C.!

Is it becoming apparent to you, as it has to me, that Jesus perhaps does relate more to Native people than we give Him credit for?

He knows what Native people have gone through, what suffering minority people face at the hands of dominant societies, and views life not only from a heavenly perspective, but through the eyes of an oppressed people! That's the Jesus of the Bible!

Let me bring out one other aspect for our consideration from the teachings of Scripture that relates very much to Indian people.

Though many view Christianity as the "Whiteman's Religion," we need to see that we Native people have much in common with the Israelites. All the way from Old Testament practices, which parallel Indian traditional forms of worship and rituals, to the practice of creation worship versus Creator worship. This has both positive and negative ramifications.

It is positive in the sense that Native people have so much in common culturally with the Israelites, the people group from whom the gospel originated. We really shouldn't feel like we are "aliens" to this message. This is an important truth, that will hopefully help the Body of Christ become more effective and relevant to our people. I will further develop this truth in another chapter.

It is negative in the sense that we have followed the same path that the Israelites did as they changed the glory of the incorruptible God into images made like to corruptible man, four-footed beasts, creeping things, etc. They fell away from their Creator by substituting a golden calf, etc., for the one true God. We, too, have done the same thing.

It cannot be denied that there are tremendous parallels between the Old Testament Hebrews and the traditional ways of ancestral aboriginal people of this land.

I have been studying an interesting book on the history of my tribe, originally published in 1885 by William Warren, entitled "History of the Ojibwa Nation." Our tribe goes by three different names. You can call us Ojibwa, Chippewa, or, as we refer to ourselves, Anishinabe. In this book, the author, who was part Ojibwa, states:

> *The writer has learned enough of the religion of the Ojibwas to strengthen his belief of the analogy with the Hebrews. They assert that the Me-da-we rite was granted them by the Great Spirit in a time of trouble and death, through the intercession of Man-ab-osho, the universal uncle of the An-ish-in-aub-ag. Certain rules to guide their course in life were given them at the same time, and are represented in hieroglyphics. These great rules of life, which the writer has often heard inculcated by the Me-da-we initiators in their secret teachings to their novices, bear a strong likeness to the ten commandments revealed by the Almighty to the children of Israel, amidst the awful lightning and thunder on Mount Sinai.*
>
> *They have a tradition telling of a great pestilence, which suddenly cut off many while encamped in one great village. They were saved by one of their number, to whom a spirit in the shape of a serpent discovered a certain root, which to this day they name the Ke-na-big-wushk or snakeroot. The songs and rites of this medicine are*

incorporated in the Me-da-we. The above circumstances is told to have happened when the "earth was new," and taking into consideration the lapse of the ages, and their being greatly addicted to figurative modes of expression, this tradition bears some resemblance to the plague of the children of Israel in the wilderness, which was stopped by means of the brazen serpent of Moses.

The Ojibwa pin-jig-o-saun, or as we term it, "medicine bag," contains all which he holds most sacred; it is preserved with great care, and seldom ever allowed a place in the common wigwam, but is generally left hanging in the open air on a tree, where even an ignorant child dare not touch it. The contents are never displayed without much ceremony. This, too, however distant, still bears some analogy to the receptacle of the Holy of Holies of the Hebrews.[1]

Warren goes on to say

To satisfy my own curiosity I have sometimes interpreted to their old men, portions of Bible history, and their expression invariably: "the book must be true, for our ancestors have told us similar stories, generation after generation, since the earth was new. It is a bold assertion, but it is nevertheless a true one, that were traditions of the Ojibwas written in order, and published in a book, it would as a whole bear a striking resemblance to the Old Testament.[2]

Scripture itself once again seems to speak to Indian people as the Apostle Paul explains to the Romans how ancestral people (including the Hebrews) moved from Creator worship to creation worship.

The wrath of God is being revealed from heaven against all the godlessness and wickedness of men who suppress the truth by their wickedness, since what may be known about God is plain to them, because God has made it plain to them. For since the creation of the world God's invisible qualities, his eternal power and divine nature, have been clearly seen, being understood from what has been made, so that men are without excuse. For although they knew God, they neither glorified him as God nor gave thanks to him, but their thinking became futile and their foolish hearts were darkened. Although they claimed to be wise they became fools, and exchanged the glory of the immortal God for images made to look like mortal man and birds and animals and reptiles. Romans 1:18-23

Indian people, like the children of Israel, fell away from the Creator by worshiping the creation instead.

Exchanging the glory of the immortal God for images made to look like mortal man, birds, animals and reptiles are a common part of many religions of the world. This includes many of the ancestral ways of the aboriginal people of North America. When God's highest creation looks to creation rather than the Creator for spiritual guidance and direction, and even worship such created forms, an inverted form of pure worship and spiritual guidance is the end result.

When God made man, He made man as the highest form of creation, with a specific purpose to give his Creator the highest form of praise and adoration. Man is above the rest of God's creation, and when he substitutes lower forms of creation for the Creator as the object of reverence and worship and spiritual guidance, he is rearranging God's divine order of creation, placing lower levels of creation up above the highest level of creation, and we end up worshiping objects that we were to have authority and rule over.

The Biblical account of man's creation clearly shows this:

So God created man in his own image, in the image of God he created him; male and female he created them. God blessed them and said to them, "be fruitful and increase in number; fill the earth and subdue it. Rule over the fish of the sea, and the birds of the air and over every living creature that moves on the ground." Genesis 1:27-28

We do a disservice to our own status as created beings made in the image of God, which no other aspect of creation can boast, when we elevate over us lower levels of creation as objects of worship and reverence, and from whom we receive a guiding spirit for our life. It diminishes the sanctity and special relationship God has between Himself and His highest level of creation, you and me!

When the biblical and historical facts are analyzed, it makes it very difficult to justify the argument that Jesus Christ is a white man, and the message of Christianity is the Whiteman's Gospel.

The facts just don't support this claim.

What honest biblical and historical studies confirm is that God, in His Almighty knowledge and wisdom, allowed the Savior of the world, His Son, Jesus Christ, to be born into a culture that scored the lowest grade of any people group, whether it is regarding numerical power, advanced culture and human strength and enablement or in terms of acceptance by the rest of the world.

In many ways the Indian people of North America can easily relate to such a people group. We too, have suffered at the hands of a dominant society which committed all forms of atrocities against ancestral Native forbearers, and ours has been a literal struggle for survival. Yet we, like the Israelites, have refused over the years to either conform to the ways around us or be done in by powers stronger than us.

We know from further biblical study that the gospel of Jesus Christ started among His own people, the Israelites, but the message of salvation through Jesus Christ was a message that was to be taken to the entire world, for the entire world was in need of a Savior.

We understand the gospel best as a missionary movement. The concept of spreading religious belief to other people with intense fervor is a concept easily accepted and understood by those of us who are called Christians worldwide, but runs counter to the psyche and religious teaching of Indians who are in traditional Indian religions.

Most Indian people, while having tremendous zeal and commitment to whatever traditional religion they hold to, usually don't see their calling as making their religion a missionary movement. In fact, just the opposite is often true.

Many true traditionalists become upset at the number of non-Indian people, such as those associated with the New Age Movement, who have begun to incorporate Indian spirituality with their own new fangled beliefs. In fact, it would be wrong to suggest that the majority of Indian people want their religious practices to extend outside the parameters of Indian people themselves.

We in the Body of Christ who minister among Indian people must understand this inherent difference of understanding that builds the canyon dividing Indians and others. We as obedient Christians must obey the Great Commission that Jesus gave in Matthew:

> *Then Jesus came to them and said, "all authority in heaven and on earth has been given to me. Therefore, go and make disciples of all nations, baptizing them in the name of the Father and of the Son, and of the Holy Spirit." Matthew 28:18-19*

The traditional Indian does not have such a commission in his religious mandate, and subsequently does not fully comprehend and understand the strong motivating force Christians have in propagating the gospel to the cultures of the world. Also, they normally don't appreciate having their religious practices, which have been handed down from generation to generation, called into question and told by outsiders that there is only one way, the Jesus way.

Though it doesn't diminish the truth of the gospel one bit, many overly zealous, culturally insensitive people have shot off their gospel gun in reservation after reservation in such a way that gives no room for sensitivity and understanding of how the people they are targeting to reach view their own Native spirituality and outside religious issues.

The Bible reminds us that after Jesus ascended to heaven, His followers began to spread the message of the cross and resurrection to "none but the Jews only." It wasn't until Peter in Acts chapter 10, was instructed by the Holy Spirit himself to reach out beyond just the Jews to the Gentile world. When he did, he met with great opposition from the Jewish Christian leadership, until finally they truly caught the vision and the missionary enterprise of the early church began in earnest.

Up to this point, I have taken great care to try and draw the comparison between Native Americans and the Jews, in terms of our cultural similarities. Let me also note here, though, that there are lessons on how not to act as we see how Israel began to spread the gospel of Christ. We need to see that Israel was guilty of cultural elitism in the early days of the spread of the gospel, with many, including their religious leaders, feeling that the message of the gospel was for them and them alone. Sharing Christ with the Gentiles was not even considered by some to be their mandate, though Christ clearly included them in His Great Commission.

When Israel finally realized that the gospel was to spread from them to all the nations of the world and they began to share Christ from that understanding, people of many countries and traditions turned to Christ and followed His teachings.

Included eventually in the spread of the gospel were the people groups of what we now know as Europe, from where the white man had his ancestral homeland, and from where the influx of European immigrants to this land originated.

What many Native North Americans and white men fail to understand is that prior to the introduction of Christianity into the cultures of Europe, most Europeans were involved in the same kind of animistic forms of worship common among Native American tribes, the Israelites, and others who embrace spirit worship worldwide as alluded to previously in Romans 1:18-23!

Spirit worship abounded, and animism and witchcraft were the hallmarks of ancient European religions. That is, until redemption through the shed blood of Jesus Christ came. In fact, Christianity is the only "religion" in the history of the world that has offered true freedom from the effects of animistic worship, which is based on fear. Relationship with Jesus Christ truly offers all of us lasting hope.

Most contemporary documentaries and writings of and about Native people present Native spirituality in exclusively a positive light, describing it in some familiar terms such as "Native spirituality is being harmonious with nature," etc. What is often hidden from Hollywood's cameras and the modern writer's pen is the other side of animism, which includes dark and often fearful deals with the spirit world, and constantly living in a world of fear, always trying to appease that kingdom of darkness.

Though there are many beautiful and positive things about

Native cultures, those who are steeped deeply in Native spiritism have to admit that there is this darker side, which is often not mentioned nor fully understood by those who look through naive eyes from the outside at Native cultures and religions.

It bears to be said time and time again that, for the white man, as well as a Native person, to accept Christ and Christianity is to accept something that was foreign to him, but is the only remedy to the fear problem associated with animistic practices. The gospel began with Israel, a minority, tribal and oppressed people, in a place called Palestine, and eventually reached the European countries, and eventually made its way to the new world.

Anglo Americans must also see themselves as products of missions, unless they have Jewish blood in their background. If someone had not brought the gospel to their ancestral people, many would not be Christian today. The white man is not the author of Christianity. God is. The white man only happened to be the messenger to bring the gospel to this part of the world. Interestingly, as we approach the twenty-first century, God seems to be turning to other people groups to lead the Body of Christ in missionary involvement around the globe today.

Indian people have had contact with Christianity basically only for the past few hundred years, and from within this context. Redemption through Jesus Christ has been in existence for nearly two thousand years. Most of the contact Indian people have had with the messengers of this message has been basically the white, Anglo Saxon people from Europe. For that reason, and that reason alone, Indian people have equated Christianity with the white man, and hence, the concept developed that it's the Whiteman's Gospel.

The realization that God chose a minority, tribal group of people to bring salvation to the world and reconciliation between God and his creation is not normally the way Native people view Christianity. But this is the truth. The gospel is not the "Whiteman's Gospel!" He didn't invent it, he didn't start it, he didn't author it! ✄

God, in his infinite wisdom chose a people group so similar to the Native North Americans, that it's hard for me to see why more Native North Americans don't accept this plan of salvation.

That God chose an oppressed, minority, tribal people group to bring the Savior of the world to mankind begs the question, "Why?"

The simple answer, I believe, is that God delights to use the underdog!

And that opens up a world of possibilities for minorities and oppressed people around the world, if we would only submit ourselves to the righteousness which is of God, and reach our potential in impacting the world with a positive message of reconciliation through Christ.

Careful biblical and historical studies point to the fact that God has often used the most unsuspecting ones to be chosen people for chosen purposes. There seems to be a divine reason for this. As I studied the Word of God with this idea in mind, I was amazed to see how time and time again, He used the insignificant of the world to do his greatest work.

This truth is also of utmost importance to us as Native Christians as we seek to be used of God.

Let me explain.

1   William Warren, *History of the Ojibway Nation* (Ross & Haines, Inc., Minneapolis, MN) Reprinted 1970 Pages 67-68

2   Ibid, Page 71

Chapter 2

God
and the
Underdogs

I BELIEVE THAT the reason God has chosen, throughout the history of mankind, to use the underdogs to do his greatest work is very simple. It is so that no man or people group would receive the credit.

A look back historically shows that God used underdogs, individually, collectively, alone, or as a part of a nation to accomplish some mighty impossible tasks.

As already mentioned, the Savior of the world was revealed to humanity through probably one of the most insignificant, underrated, over abused and mistreated people groups in the history of the world, the Israelites.

Individually, God used insignificant ones, like the little shepherd boy, David, to bring Goliath and the enemy to their knees, to the surprise of the mighty armies of both sides.

In the New Testament, the pattern continues.

In Luke chapter 10, we read that the Lord appointed seventy-two individuals who were given the job description of going before Him and preparing the way for his arrival. They were to go into communities, and announce that the "kingdom of God is near you" (Luke 10:9).

In Luke 10:17, we read, *The seventy-two returned with joy and said, "Lord, even the demons submit to us in your name!"*

As Jesus reflected on the good report of the seventy-two, He looked to heaven and offered a prayer of thanksgiving to His Father. He said in Luke 10:21,

I praise you Father, Lord of heaven and earth, because you have hidden these things from the wise and learned, and revealed them to little children. Yes, Father, for this was your good pleasure.

Who were these seventy-two that Christ chose to do this task?

He avoided the temptation that many people of our day fall prey to, that of looking for the "big name" people to do the work. Think of all the wonderful publicity He would have had if He had some people with name recognition doing this task. We often fall prey to this temptation, by thinking our efforts will be enhanced if we can only secure the endorsement or involvement of the star athletes, or celebrities to join our cause, or if we can get those who can influence, or have financial resources to stand shoulder to shoulder with us.

Yes, He probably would have had the publicity, but He probably would have been lacking in results! And that, unfortunately, is all too often what happens in our day.

There is, what I believe, a spiritual principle that needs to be brought back to our attention these days. That is the principle of God using underdogs to do His greatest and most effective work. If the church would only understand and act on this principle, how much more effective would we be in these days!

The seventy-two that Jesus chose were not looked upon by those around them as special, just a bunch of average, everyday kind of people who would never have sought, nor have wanted the spotlight of the world on them.

What they did possess, however, was an intense level of faithfulness, motivated by a sense of inadequacy and complete dependence on God's empowering. Jesus told them to do certain things, and in the course of their faithfulness to their duties, God gave them even more favor, allowing them to deal with the demonic forces that were arrayed against them during that day. These demonic forces provided the motivation for all sorts of wicked and vile living. So the seventy-two were not only paving the way for Christ's visits to these communities, they were confronting and defeating the very powers that were at the root of all the evil in those communities.

I would suggest that the reason these underdogs were successful, above and beyond their call of duty, was that they weren't preoccupied with thoughts about how their high status in life allowed them the privilege of being called by the Lord for this task. They were not concerned about how being chosen by Christ would have favorable impact on their lives and somehow help them climb some imaginary ladder of success in the ministry.

I note with interest what the Lord said to the disciples after this event occurred. He says privately to them in verses 23-24,

> *Blessed are the eyes that see what you see. For I tell you that many prophets and kings wanted to see what you see but did not see it, and to hear what you hear but did not hear it.*

Jesus says that many mighty and noble people would love to experience with their eyes and ears, what the disciples just had the privilege of experiencing, that of the spiritual achievements of the underdogs.

God seems to, historically, reserve special revelations of Himself and His ways for the disenfranchised and those who have been oppressed. He seems to delight in reserving special revelations of His ways and means to those whom the rest of the world views as "second class citizens."

But not only are the seventy-two, sent out by Jesus, the only ones listed in the New Testament as examples of underdogs. The New Testament includes the underdogs of Corinth and of our own day.

In I Corinthians 1:26-29 we read,

> *Brothers, think of what you were when you were called. Not many of you were wise by human standards; not many were influential; not many were of noble birth. But God chose the foolish things of the world to shame the wise; God chose the weak things of the world to shame the strong. He chose the lowly things of the world and the*

despised things—and the things that are not —to nullify the things that are, so that no one may boast before Him.

This passage points out a few major considerations for us as we discuss the implications of being considered underdogs.

First, we must realize that God does not exclude anyone from salvation, nor from being used of Him. He says "not many of you were wise by human standards; not many were influential; not many of noble birth."

God's gospel is for all people, and as each one of us comes to Christ, we come to Him with personal histories and life experiences that are as different as the colors of the rainbow. Some are from noble birth, or possess great wisdom (by human standards), or have the natural ability to influence (meaning economically, politically, socially, etc.). But Scripture reminds us that the numbers of those who hold such status are "not many." Those who have it all often have a strong sense of self sufficiency, and are needing to be in control of all the affairs of their lives. That's why it's so hard for such people to sense their need of salvation. This led Jesus to comment that it's easier for a camel to go through the eye of a needle than for a rich man to enter heaven.

Secondly, we are reminded from this passage that the standards of evaluation being used here are human standards and not heavenly standards.

Mankind has always had classes in cultures, usually being defined as the "haves and have nots." Or, as we have often heard, the "upper crust." My definition of the "upper crust" is basically a bunch of crumbs held together by their own dough!

It must be understood that when Scripture says, God chooses the "foolish, weak, and lowly," it does not mean that this is how God sees people. What it says is that God has chosen the foolish, weak and lowly who are classified as such by human standards.

God does not look at humanity through "glasses of classes," nor does He endorse, necessarily, the human standards that we evaluate other people by.

In fact, Scripture reminds us that God is no respecter of persons. With Him, there is neither Jew nor Greek, slave nor free, male nor female, for you are all one in Christ. The body of Christ is made up of people from both sides of the tracks, and all of us bring to our calling as faithful followers of Christ very unique and different experiences and priorities that can be used by God.

Another truth in this passage relates to the reason God delights to use underdogs. He says in verse 29, "so that no one may boast before Him."

It's clear that when God does great work through underdogs, they can't look to themselves or their past, or their power as the reason why this great work was done. God does not want to share His glory with mankind! He used underdogs in the past, and He still desires to use underdogs in the present, and He will use underdogs in the future, so that all of the praise and adoration will go to Himself, and Himself alone!

The underdog brings to the table of availability for service in the Lord's work a unique perspective on life, priorities, and what's important. Those from the higher and more "successful" classes of people may have these qualities, but in my opinion, they have to work harder at not being puffed up, wanting to take credit for things of the Spirit, or confusing their own enablements and abilities for the dynamic working of the Holy Spirit in their lives.

Underdogs come at it differently. Most underdogs don't have a track record of success and victory. For most underdogs, just the opposite is true.

This brings us to the question of how this applies to us as Native North Americans when we become Christians and seek to please God by our lives and service for Christ? How do we see ourselves, and how does the rest of society, and even the Body of Christ see us?

How We View Ourselves

Back in the early 1970s my father was asked to serve as the president of the Mokahum Indian Bible School, a Christian and Missionary Alliance training school located on my home reservation. The campus was situated about five miles northwest of the community of Cass Lake.

It was a small school, with usually only a handful of Native students registered each year. Some were studying to enter full time ministry, while others were desiring biblical studies to help them in their daily walk with Christ.

My dad shared with me a story from those days that illustrates the challenge we face in helping our people move beyond their sense of inadequacy and feeling of "second classness," in comparison to the rest of society.

Many of the students that attended the Bible School were from backgrounds that were not very positive. Many who committed their lives to Christ did so coming out of pasts that included alcoholism, abuse and despair. Building self confidence was one of the major challenges facing the teachers and staff.

Dad recalls that once he and a student had to go to Minneapolis to pick up an item that had been donated to the school. They went to the big city in the school van, pulling a trailer which would be used to bring this large item home.

They had to go right into the heart of the city to pick up this item. As they passed by skyscraper after skyscraper, the student's amazement could not be contained.

"Boy, just look at these tall buildings!" he said with eyes and mouth wide open. "Just look at all the things that the white man can build and all that he can accomplish!"

He went on and on, pouring on such adulation and reverence for those who were so intelligent and smart, and who seemed to possess such incredible abilities that we as Indian people surely didn't have.

This kind of story can be told time and time again, among many Native people. It can be told because many Native people have a very low image of themselves and their people when compared to the dominant society of our land. I call it the Indian car syndrome.

The Indian car syndrome illustrates the way many Native people use our unique humor in expressing painful views of ourselves, and what our expectations of ourselves are.

One missionary among Indians once commented, "Indian people are the most stoic people I have ever seen. They seldom laugh, and seem to have no sense of humor whatsoever." I don't know where this missionary served, but his statement can be nothing farther from the truth.

The truth is, Native people have one of the most amazing and hilarious senses of humor that I have ever observed among any people group I have encountered, worldwide! Again, the comparison can be made between the Native American and the Jewish people. Who are some of the most popular and top humorists in America today? Many of them are Jewish. Humor is, for an oppressed people, one of the most powerful tools to deal with the pain and agony you face. For Indians, humor is a way of life. It's a survival tool. It's what has enabled us to endure. In many ways, Native humor mirrors that of Jewish humor.

Just what is an Indian car? An Indian car is always two colors. Red and rust, blue and rust, green and rust, or white and rust. An Indian car can be easily identified a mile away from the tell tale blue smoke that rises from underneath the body of the car. Red tape has replaced the red turn signal lens, and if you need parts for your Indian car, no problem. Just go in the back yard and choose from the six other Indian cars up on blocks for whatever you need. Oh, one other rule for owning an Indian car. You can wash the outside of the windows as many times as you want, but you must never wash the insides of the windows for as long as you own the vehicle. Also, why is an Indian car always so low to the ground? That is a natural phenomenon that normally happens when you place more than fifteen individuals in one vehicle.

The joke that used to go around our community was this, "Did you hear about the one car rollover on the reservation the other day? Forty-two people were hurt!"

It's not just cars that get the designation "Indian" when they are in this state. I visited a Native neighbor in my hometown shortly after my marriage. When I entered their home, we had a great laugh at what they called their "Indian TV." It was a beautiful twenty-five inch color console set, but when you turned it on only about five inches of the center part of the screen were visible, and that was black and white!

The Indian church I attended had what we called an "Indian coffee maker." You know, one of the thirty cup machines most churches have. Ours however, had the handle missing. It made great coffee, but in order to get some out of the container, you had to use a needle-nose pliers to reach into the hole where the handle used to be, and twist up the mechanism to get anything out! We called that an "Indian coffee pot!"

I love good Indian humor. We can take the worst of ourselves, and find a way to laugh about it. "I just had to laugh," is one of the most common phases used back home. But what really is behind the humor? What are we really saying about ourselves, when we label things that don't work well with the label "Indian?"

What we really are saying beyond the laughing is this—to be Indian is not good, and anything broken down and not working is equated with ourselves. We are saying that we are not good, we are broken down, we are not working well. Humor only hides the true painful and low feelings many Native people have about themselves. We continue to hurt from the loss of our lands, cultures, languages, and ways, over the past few hundred years. We often try to soften that hurt through our humor.

It is clear that there have been many factors that have contributed to this mentality. The negative impact the government and church run boarding schools had on our people around the turn of this century stands as a major factor in producing negative attitudes, but there were other issues that contributed to this state of mind.. The disintegration of traditional culture brought on by the confinement on reservations and the inability of tribal cultures to continue a hunting and gathering way of life in a rapidly changing social environment brought on by European settlement and colonization was equally as impacting a force as the boarding schools were.

This negative mentality is not the historical view of ourselves that our ancestors and forefathers had. We were once a proud people, a generous people, and a considerate, and caring people. But we must also confess that not all the traditions and historical ways of our ancestors were blameless and without a fault.

Even in my own tribe, the Chippewa, or Ojibwa, our history is one of great triumph and great tragedy. Even the name "Ojibwa," reminds me that we were not as kind and compassionate as we should have been, especially in the way we apparently treated our captured enemies.

In his book, *The History of the Ojibwa Nation*, William Warren shares how we probably got that name.

> *The word is composed of O-jib, "pucker up", and ub-way, "to roast," and it means "To roast till puckered up."*
>
> *It is well authenticated by their traditions, and by the writings of their early white discoverers, that before they became acquainted with, and made use of the fire arm and other European deadly weapons of war, instead of their primitive bow and arrow and war-club, their wars with other tribes were less deadly, and they were more accustomed to secure captives, whom under uncontrolled feeling incited by aggravated wrong, and revenge for similar injuries, they tortured by fire in various ways.*
>
> *The name of Au-boin-ug (roasters), which the Ojibwas have given to the Dahcotas or Sioux, originated in their roasting their captives, and it is as likely that the word Ojibwa (to roast till puckered up), originated in the same manner.*[1]

According to the most recent census information, Native North Americans and Aleuts comprise less than one percent of the modern North American population. Less than one percent! We are at the bottom of the totem pole numerically, socially, economically (except for the few who are bringing in huge per capita payments from their local casinos) in comparison to the rest of America. All that doesn't discourage me, though, it encourages me!

Why, you might ask? All these seemingly negative challenges facing us as Native people clearly qualify us for the designation, "underdog!" And hasn't it been shown that historically, God's greatest work has been done by the underdogs?

How Others View Us

But not only do we look inwardly to see how we view ourselves. To get the complete picture, we need to look outwardly and examine how the rest of society views Native Americans, and more importantly and relevant to our discussion, how has the Church seen us, and how has it organized its ministry among us both historically, and contemporarily?

Author and Indian advocate Vine Deloria, Jr., summed up his view of how those from outside Indian society see our people.

Indians are like the weather. Everyone knows all about the weather, but none can change it. When storms are predicted, the sun shines. When picnic weather is announced, the rain begins. Likewise, if you count on the unpredictability of Indian people, you will never be sorry.

One of the finest things about being an Indian is that people are always interested in you and your "plight." Other groups have difficulties, predicaments, quandaries, problems, or troubles. Traditionally, we Indians have had a "plight."

Our foremost plight is our transparency. People can tell just by looking at us what we want, what should be done to help us, how we feel, and what a "real" Indian is really like. Indian life, as it relates to the real world, is a continuous attempt not to disappoint people who know us. Unfulfilled expectations cause grief and we have already had our share.

Because people can see right through us, it becomes impossible to tell truth from fiction or fact from mythology. Experts paint us as they would like us to be. Often we paint ourselves as we wish we were or as we might have been.

The more we try to be ourselves, the more we are forced to defend what we have never been. The American public feels most comfortable with the mythical Indians of stereotype-land who were always THERE. These Indians are fierce, they wear feathers and grunt. Most of us don't fit this idealized figure since we grunt only when overeating, which is seldom.

To be an Indian in modern American society is in a very real sense to be unreal and ahistorical.[2]

How true it is that those outside our culture tend to view our people in a continued, stereotypical fashion, which is for the most part, inaccurate, and all too often condescending.

In our years of traveling and visiting numerous churches across North America we have had our own full share of some of the most amazing and outlandish remarks by non-Indians about Indian people.

I remember one time after a concert in a local church, we were back at our sales table selling our music tapes, when an older gentleman approached us and began looking over our wares. My wife, LaDonna, was standing with me when this man, reaching for one of our tapes, shared with us that he was completely positive that his grandfather had to have been an Indian, because "he had that, you know, big nose and bags under his eyes."

After years of hearing such comments, I have tried to keep my mouth shut in responding to these kinds of statements, but sometimes my wife will still share verbally what I'm thinking internally!

She looked him straight in his baggy eyes and big nose and commented, "Well sir, how do you know that he wasn't just a clumsy white man who fell down and broke his nose and since that fall suffers from insomnia?"

There I was muttering under my breath, "Leave him alone, he's going to buy a tape!"

He looked LaDonna straight in her not so baggy eyes and cute little nose and replied, "Well Ma'am, I never thought of that!" He never did buy a tape. He just put it down and walked away in deep contemplation!

Another time we were being entertained at a restaurant after a service somewhere in the Midwest, when our host commented to us that he was sure his grandmother was an Indian because she had those "beady little eyes!"

Once again, LaDonna came to the rescue, and she leaned a bit over the table toward this gentleman and said, "We all have those beady little eyes!"

One experience though, lives in my memory as one of the cutest exchanges I have ever had in my life.

While in a local church in Tennessee, I was speaking at a missions conference. I was asked to go to the public elementary school and speak to several classes about Native Americans. I went into one first grade class, and began to share with about thirty students about Native Americans. Their eyes were riveted on me as I showed them some of my regalia, including my non-Chippewa headdress (but who will ever know!), and other items.

As I began to speak to the class, a young blond haired, blue-eyed first grader put his hand up, and waved it at me with great excitement. He kept it up so long, that he had to brace it up with his other hand, so I felt I better let this young man ask his question.

After I asked him to share his question, he responded with the biggest smile I had ever seen, and pronounced with great enthusiasm, "I'm an Indian!"

"You are?" I commented back to him. And then I asked him a question that he was definitely not ready for. I said, "What tribe are you from?"

His smile turned to great trepidation, until what he thought was a good answer came to him.

"Cleveland!" he shouted back at me with a mixture of excitement and relief in his voice!

It reminds me of a poster I saw once, hanging in an office of the Indian Center in the city of Chicago. The poster had four sports banners on it, representing three imaginary and one real major league team. The first banner was for the "Kansas City Caucasians," the second was for the "New York Negroes," the third was for the "Pittsburgh Jews," and the fourth one was for the "Cleveland Indians." I guess that says it all, when it comes to why many Native people have risen up in protest to the many stereotyped images of our people that professional sports continues to portray, and how incomprehensible it would be to name teams after any other culture of people, even though it's O.K. to do it to the Native Americans.

In America today, there are a multitude of mostly romanticized views and beliefs, by the dominant society, and even by other minority groups, about the Native Americans. Most of those views do portray us, when compared to the dominant society, as underdogs, and the ones who must be the recipients of the benevolence of those who are stronger, wealthier, and in a position to "help" those who are "less fortunate" than themselves.

What it really boils down to is that the value systems and world views of the dominant society and that of minority cultures (including Native North American), are inheritantly different, and those value systems motivate us in what we do.

A perfect example of this happened to my wife and I back in 1987, at a church gathering in St. Paul, Minnesota.

We had made our way to some open seats on the main floor of the auditorium. After locating those seats, we sat down next to an older couple that we had not met before. With about twenty minutes to go before the service began, we started up a conversation with the couple who sat next to us.

After sharing the normal small talk, we found out that this couple were missionaries, serving for a number of years in a foreign land. We shared that we were Native Americans, and mentioned to them our tribal affiliations. When this couple learned that LaDonna was a Navajo, their countenance changed from interested to, what I can only describe as intense pity for the young lady sitting next to them.

He took LaDonna by the hand, embracing it and patting it with as much emotion as he could, and shared, "Ohhhhhh, we've traveled through the Navajo reservation, and, ohhhhhh, we've seen those little mud huts, and, ohhhhhhhh, it's so sad to see just how those people have to live....." Ohhhhh, he almost had me in tears and feeling sorry for her, too!

LaDonna's response, true to her personality was probably shocking, to say the least to this veteran missionary.

"What do you mean, it's so sad to see the Navajos living that way?" she said, in her own gentle but strong way.

"They love it!" she said. "They don't have a mortgage payment, and their utility bills don't face them every month, and their grocery store is out back in the sheep corral!"

How often ministry to those of other cultures has been shaped and attempted by the value systems of those bringing the gospel cross-culturally, and not through the value system of those intended to be reached. I think the point needs to be made that though value systems are different from one culture to another that does not necessarily make them less, or not as good as those values with which we are comfortable.

This lesson is one that has to be continually taught to all of us, no matter from what culture we come from. It happens here in America, as well as around the world wherever cross-cultural ministry is engaged in.

I can still recall vividly an experience I had with several other Native American brothers as we were visiting the country of Mongolia. At the time of our visit, the church was only about four years old, and the initial few believers in that country had multiplied to well more than a thousand. We were thrilled to be in local churches there where the vast majority of believers were under the age of twenty. It was exciting to go to the more isolated parts of that country, close to the Russian border, where the people live nomadically, and share Christ with those who had never heard of him before.

Our delegation was invited to the apartment of one of the American missionary couples in the capital city of UlanBaatar who was involved in ministry there. There were several young American couples who joined us for a time of fellowship, and the discussion turned to how their ministries were going.

One couple, I recall, were sharing their intense frustration with their work, which was geared to helping Mongols develop industry and businesses.

Their frustration centered around the fact that they could not get the Mongol people to be to work on time at 8:00 a.m. and stay till the 5:00 p.m. closing time. They would show up for work when they wanted, and leave when they wanted. I recall asking this couple how long they had been involved in their work in the country and they said, "for about a month." Our counsel to this couple was simple, but later they shared with us privately that it was to them, very profound. This couple was attempting, in a very short time frame, to impose an outside value system, as it relates to employment and business, that the Mongol people were not accustomed to. We shared with them that perhaps they were trying to impose an "Americanized" value system that they were unable to, at that time, relate to, nor embrace. We shared with them that what they really needed to do was to learn how the Mongol people culturally do things, and attempt to adapt their American approach to fit that culture. There definitely needed to be changes, but the American couple automatically felt that the change needed to be from the Mongol way to that of their way, and not the other way around. The movement and change really needed to be on the part of the American couple to that of the Mongol value system, if they were ever to have an effect on the people they were attempting to help.

It is also true that we as Native North Americans also have stereotypical views about those from other races and cultures. It really is a problem that is not limited to just one culture or one race of people. It is found wherever there are people of a different upbringing and values. The challenge we face today is being open minded enough and willing to move from our cultural comfort zones to learn about and from one another, and to have an appreciation for cultures and ways that are not the same as ours.

I thank God that we are now seeing this movement beginning to happen from both sides of the cultural fence in what can only be described as an unprecedented awakening in the Body of Christ and in North American history. We are living in what is becoming an era of one of the most potentially positive days for both the church and Native people, and all people of color for that matter.

In no small way, God is once again demonstrating his delight in using the most unsuspecting ones, the underdogs, to do His greatest work through. What I am speaking of is the way He has used the Promise Keepers organization to be the spiritual wrecking ball on walls that have existed for centuries.

From their incredibly powerful "Stand in the Gap" solemn assembly of hundreds of thousands of men on the mall in Washington, D.C., on October 4, 1997 to their stadium conferences which have drawn millions, and even through personal visits of their leaders to a number of reservations across America, the message of Promise Keepers and reconciliation is resonating with Native men, and the Native church.

I think, for one of the first times in the history of Christianity among Native people, the message of the Cross is not being distorted or diminished by the methods that removed its credibility. Real Christian love, repentance, forgiveness, and inclusiveness of all people has always been biblical truth, but finally, after nearly five centuries of the gospel being here in North America, is it being demonstrated in a way that has never been seen before. Native people exposed to the message of Promise Keepers are embracing it, and seeing what it really means to demonstrate biblical humility, love and acceptance.

The work God has begun to do in North America through Promise Keepers must be carried on, and God must be allowed to continue awakening and shaping the church into the end time army He wants it to be.

Both the Anglo and the Native communities have before us one of the greatest opportunities to capitalize on what the Spirit of God is doing in making us, as Jesus prayed in John 17, united and one. We must not miss this opportunity to correct the mistakes of the past, ask and grant forgiveness and pray for healing for each other today, and set the course for the future with eyes looking to Jesus who is the author and finisher of not only our faith, but the perfector of His Body.

To God be the glory, great things He has done! And wouldn't you know it? True to His ways, He did it through another underdog. Are there any other underdogs out there that God wants to use who would be willing to step out and obey? Are we listening? Are we hearing God's voice? Are we awake to this reality? Couldn't you just imagine what might happen if a few more underdogs were willing to stand up and be counted!

1   William Warren, *History of the Ojibway Nation* (Ross & Haines, Inc., Minneapolis, MN) Reprinted 1970 Page 36

2   Vine Deloria, Jr., *Custer Died for Your Sins* (University of Oklahoma Press) Third Printing 1989 Pages 1-2

Chapter 3

Christianity
and
Indian History

THE MOST IMPORTANT question that needs to be addressed in this book is how has the Church viewed Native people, historically, and contemporarily. This is more important to me than how the general public views our people, and what will have the greatest impact on how ministry is conducted among Native North Americans.

For you see, not only are Native people guilty of misinterpreting the gospel as the "Whiteman's Gospel," but I believe that, unknowingly, the dominant society has often embraced and fostered the mentality that it is their gospel. History points to this reality.

The potential for this mindset is still a real possibility today, and at times is evident even through the hallowed halls of ecclesiastical hierarchy. The ownership of the power and control of most ministry in the United States and Canada, and ultimately, around the world is still, by and large, handled exclusively within the Anglo American community, though constituencies may be multi-cultural.

I share these thoughts not to condemn, but hopefully to help the Body of Christ see how those from outside the culture, that hold the power and control of much of the ministry efforts of the contemporary church worldwide, see this issue. My hope and prayer is that the Church would be willing to see itself as others do, and address areas of needed change. I pray that it will also be willing to adjust its basic assumptions of the people it attempts to reach, worldwide, in order to be as effective in reaching them as it could and must be in these last days.

In order for us to understand why Native North Americans have become so resistant to the gospel, a walk back in history is necessary.

In order to dispel some stereotypical views of Native North Americans, it is important to understand that before Columbus "discovered" this land, our people were here in great numbers.

Prior to the European discovery of this land, Native North Americans numbered between eight and twelve million, and were divided up into hundreds of tribes, each one uniquely different from the next, with their own set of values, cultures, traditions, languages, and expression that were as diverse as Norwegians are from the Irish.

The stereotypical view of Native North Americans, however, is that we are all the same. We all grunt and say "how" when we see each other, and we do a great job in selling cigars at the local dime store. I remember one fellow commenting to me once that he thought we had all been killed, because that was the image that the Hollywood western movies portrayed. He was somewhat shocked when he realized that standing before him was a real live Indian.

His view of our people was actually not too far from the truth, because after several centuries had passed since Columbus' boat ride, we almost were completely wiped from the face of the earth.

Historians tell us that by 1900, our population had dwindled down from approximately twelve million to only just over two hundred thousand.

Some tribes were completely wiped out either through the Indian wars or through epidemics that spread through village after village. Our people had not developed the immune system to ward off the new diseases from Europe being introduced by the new arriving immigrants. Diseases like smallpox and others ravaged Native community after community until some tribes were completely wiped out.

But not only were we subject to disease and war, we were facing an ever increasing attack on all that was traditional about our ways and life.

What was the historical mindset of the new immigrants towards Native people?

It was the conviction of many of the new arriving immigrants that the Indian people in their Native state were considered hostile and savage. In fact, one of the "thanksgiving prayers" of the early newcomers to the New World, originally published in the 1600s was reprinted recently in the form of a Thanksgiving gospel tract by one of the leading churchmen of our day. This tract included the thanksgiving prayer to God that the settlers of the 1600s were kept from the "ravages of the savages."

In his book, *Now that the Buffalo's Gone*, author Alvin M. Josephy, Jr., says,

One of the more enduring characteristics of Indian-White relations has been the susceptibility of non-Indians to thinking about Native Americans in stereotypes...They have been regarded successively as innocent children of nature, noble savages, subhuman demons, untrustworthy thieves and murderers, stoic warriors, inferior and vanishing vestiges of the Stone Age, depraved drunkards, shiftless, lazy, humorless incompetents unable to handle their own affairs—almost anything but true to life, three dimensional men, women and children, as individualistic and human as any other people on earth.[1]

It was commonly viewed historically by the ever increasing and more powerful arriving immigrants that Native people would survive only if they submitted to the dominant society, cut their braids, dressed like the white man, lived like the white man, became Christians, and fully assimilated into the ways of the newcomers.

If they were unwilling, the only other option to this would be to push them a safe distance away from the dominant society, become isolated and rendered harmless, both physically and in their capacity to influence the dominant society, or be annihilated.

In reality, these three options were implemented over the years of the expansion of the new American and Canadian society. Many Native people were forced into assimilation, while others were herded, like animals, off a safe distance away to reservations, where they would be isolated and rendered harmless. Others, as already stated, were annihilated.

This attitude was held not only by the common man, but by government leaders as well. Listen to what Thomas Jefferson Morgan, the commissioner of Indian Affairs under U.S. President Benjamin Harrison said in the late 1800s:

"The Indians must conform to the white man's ways, peaceable if they will, forcibly if they must. They must adjust themselves to their environment, and conform their mode of living substantially to our civilization...They cannot escape it, and must either conform to it or be crushed by it."

The fastest—the only—way to assimilation, as he saw it, was to get the young Indians off their reservations, away from their benighted elders, and into white-run schools. Pretending to speak for Indian babies, Morgan told one of his audiences, "These helpless little ones cry out to us: If you leave us here to grow up in our present surroundings, what can we hope for?" ...Contrasting the doleful lot of young Indians on reservations with the blessings that would come to them with White man's education, he asked, "Shall they be disappointed? Shall their hopes be blasted?...Justice, philanthropy, patriotism, Christianity answer No! And let all the people, speaking through their representatives in Congress answer No!! Give the papoose a chance.[2]

The irony of this man and his statement is that before becoming Commissioner of Indian Affairs, he had been a public educator and a Baptist minister!

It's also interesting and somewhat painful to note that when the U.S. Government established the Indian reservation system, it was put under the Department of the Interior, whose main responsibility dealt with natural resource management, including land and animals. In fact, the Indian reservation system was patterned after the wild game reserve model established to protect animals. That seemed to be, in the minds of the government, the best way to describe and deal with the Native people of that day. We were basically no better or higher than the wild animals of the forest.

How did the Church fare, historically, as it relates to Native North Americans?

In their own somewhat romanticized view of their past, most Americans and Canadians view their national history from the understanding that when the early European immigrants came to this continent, they came to exercise their religious freedom and also began the process of introducing Christianity to the Native people. The process began in earnest quite early, shortly after the new immigrants began coming.

Through the years, the missionaries and the church played a central role in the assimilation process.

Basically, when we use the term assimilation, we are talking about the process by which one people group changes their ways, culture, etc., to that of another culture or nation. Forced assimilation, then, is the process by which those who are resistant to this change are forced into it, often with the only other option being the potential loss of their lives.

How shocked I was when I went to the dictionary recently and read the real definition of assimilation.

Assimilation

"To make like the people of a nation or other group in customs, viewpoint, character, or other attribute. The process by which immigrants or other newcomers become like the people they are around, adopting the attitudes and cultural patterns of the society into which they have come."

Did you catch that! The process by which immigrants or other newcomers become like the people they are around, adopting the attitudes and cultural patterns of the society into which they have come!

Isn't that amazing? Now, no one ever told us that when the
new immigrants came here, if they were to do it right, they were
supposed to become like us, not the other way around! Something really went wrong here. How come no one ever caught
this before? Do you think it's too late to go back and start over?

All foolishness aside, the motivation behind Christian ministry, unfortunately, was not as pure as it should have been, for it
was the belief of those engaging in historical Christian ministry
among Native people not only to evangelize, but to move Indians from the perceived state of savagery to that of a civilized
state. Everything Native was considered evil, bad and unredeem-
able. Redemption therefore, was not viewed as primarily vertical, between fallen man and his God, but predominately horizontal, between a "secondary and lesser" culture to that of a
"civilized and Christian" culture. We had to basically become
white, and forsake all things Native, to become Christians.

Even when Indians did become Christians, they still were not
safe from the ever expanding dominant society's attacks on their
own ways, languages and even lives. Some examples of this
include John Eliot's converts in Massachusetts during King Philips
War in 1675-76 were either murdered or sold into slavery. In the
late 1700s, in Lancaster, Pennsylvania, a settlement of Christian
Conestoga Indians were massacred by frontiersmen. Becoming
Christians among the Cherokees and other so called "civilized"
tribes did not keep them from experiencing their forced march
called the "Trail of Tears."

After the United States government was established, a major
mistake was made, in my estimation, as far as reaching Indian
people for Christ was concerned. It was a mistake for the government to enter into a working agreement with the various denominations and church groups to aid in the process of forced
assimilation.

The government began to rely more and more on the church
to do the task of overseeing the work of the government with
the various tribes and reservations. As missionaries and churches
were given greater roles and power across our country, the pow-

ers of the church and state became confusing, with missionary activity sometimes even being subsidized by the federal government.

In 1869, U.S. President Grant began turning over the full responsibility for the administration of the Indian agencies to American churches and missionary bodies, whose honesty and integrity far surpassed the corrupt government agents who were handling government Indian affairs across the country up to that point.

In a matter of just a couple of years after that decision by President Grant, almost seventy-five Indian agencies had been turned over to the Presbyterians, Methodists, Catholics, Lutherans, Quakers, Congregationalists, Dutch Reformed, Episcopalians, Baptists, and other denominations.

The missionaries assigned to each area were there not only to evangelize, but they also filled the office of government agent, overseeing education, and other such activities on the reservations. Their authority was backed by government troops and all things Native were forbidden. Culture, language and worldview was dismantled piece by piece and forced assimilation ensued.

It wasn't until the Hayes administration that this policy of the church and state working together was abandoned, and the government took back the responsibilities of overseeing Indian affairs.

By the turn of this century the government was pushing for continued assimilation and the era of the government boarding schools was initiated. It was at these government boarding schools where Thomas Jefferson Morgan's vision for forced assimilation was to be realized. It was at just such a boarding school where my grandparents attended.

My grandmother was from the White Earth Reservation in western Minnesota, and my grandfather's roots were on the Leech Lake Reservation in northern Minnesota, and also on the Bad River Reservation in northern Wisconsin. They were removed from their parents and sent to a government school. It was there, as my grandmother related to me when I was a child, that

she and others were physically beaten by the government workers when they were caught speaking the Ojibway language. Stories of this nature abound all across the United States and Canada.

The end result of the boarding school experience was a generation of Native people who were stripped of their identity,
and told that everything about them was bad. They were told
that there was nothing worthwhile or salvageable in their culture, and if they were to survive, they must adapt to the ways of
the dominant society. Most Native children who came out of
that tragic time in our history were not willing or able to adapt
their ways to that of the dominant society. So when a people are
led to believe their culture is bad, and they resolutely refuse to
adapt to another's culture, they end up being a people with no
culture or identity.

This breeds a defeated mentality, and is what turned a whole
generation, and generations to follow, to alcohol, to ease the
pain and suffering. That is why alcohol, according to one contemporary Indian writer, directly affects close to eighty percent
of our Native population.

It grieves me as often times even North American Christians
will give me their observations of our people, often describing
our people in such terms as unmotivated drunkards, and people
who will never amount to anything, never giving thought as to
why they are in such a state, and what factors have contributed
to the many social and spiritual ills facing many Native people
today.

While the church was busy in its Indian mission work, con-
verting the souls of Native Americans, little concern was evident as to the racial and social implications that accompanied
their methods and approaches. This is probably more true among
conservative evangelicals, where the effects of the gospel on the
individual far surpass in importance the effects of the gospel on
society as a whole. This mentality leads to the inevitable priority
of, as one document suggests, "Getting people ready for the
next world replace(s) modeling the Kingdom in this one."[3]

As the Twentieth Century unfolded, there were new church

groups springing up, including independent Gospel missions, Bible societies, and Holiness Churches. New denominations including the Assemblies of God, Church of the Nazarene, Christian & Missionary Alliance, Brethren in Christ, Wesleyans, Mennonites, and others joined the mainline denominations in ministry to Native North Americans.

All throughout this time, the church was engaged in its work across Indian country. It was business as usual for most. The motivation for ministry was not to win Indian people to Christ, and allow Christ to meet the them in the midst of their culture, language and identity. Rather it was to "Americanize" as well as "Christianize" Native people.

As time went along, the governments of both America and Canada enacted various laws and acts relating to Native North Americans, and their impact is still being felt today.

In 1934, during the New Deal administration of U.S. President Franklin D. Roosevelt, the Indian Reorganization Act was passed, which among other reforms, restored to tribes freedom of religion and the right to retain and revive their own cultures.

In the 1950s, under Eisenhower's administration, the government engaged in a "termination" policy with tribes, which attempted to terminate all federal relations with tribes, end treaty obligations, and turn the reservations over to the states in which they were located. This policy was halted in 1958, however, due to the injustices and hardships suffered by the initial tribes in which this policy was imposed.

The change in policy that was initiated in 1934 under the "Indian Reorganization Act," provided the way for modern Native people to begin to "go back" to the ancestral and traditional ways of our forefathers. In fact, the 1970s became a turning point in this process. Spurred by the occupation at Wounded Knee and the rise of the Red Power Movement, there has been a revival of Native spiritualism that extends even to this day.

As you can see, historically, there have been many problems, mistakes, and atrocities committed against Native people, often in the name of Christ. This has led us to the present day challenge of righting the wrongs, as well as looking at how the gospel of Christ, which is the message of salvation to the world, can adequately be presented in the current context of the Native North American experience.

But before that can happen, I believe that the Body of Christ needs to be challenged regarding the issue of repentance for the many past hurts it has inflicted on the Native American people. Without repentance and reconciliation, Native ministry in North America will never become as effective as it should be, and I don't believe a strong Native church will have the climate in which to grow, nurture and prosper.

The challenge we face is that we must truly exercise biblical repentance and reconciliation. To be honest with you, the reconciliation movement evident in the Church today is, for me, one of the issues I approach with great fear and trepidation. I honestly do desire to be reconciled with those who have done me wrong, and I long to be reconciled with those that I have wronged. The challenge is to see that there are really two sides to the issue of reconciliation. How does reconciliation look from the other side of the tracks? Let me try and shed some light from my own perspective.

Not long ago, I was flying from my home in Glendale, Arizona to Pittsburgh, Pennsylvania to attend our denomination's annual "General Council." Accompanying me on the flight was one of our strong Native Christian leaders who has been involved in gospel ministry for almost forty years. He has been one of the few Native Christian leaders of this day who has truly had a prophetic ministry, paving the way for the next generation of leaders to follow.

He is one of the most godly men I know, and has mentored me in my ministry. I have great respect for him, and hold him in the highest esteem.

Often has been the time when he shared with me a word from the Lord in much the same way as the prophets of the Old Testament. He is a man who, like Moses, knows God face to face.

Somewhere over Kansas, we began to discuss some of the

current dialogue we have been having with the Lord.

He related the passage of Scripture to me about the Good Samaritan. He said God woke him up the previous night with this passage burning in his soul. We were flying to the denominational meeting where one of the topics to be discussed was the Native American ministries of our denomination. Native ministry and our denomination's management of it were heavy on our hearts.

He said, "God showed me last night that the biblical story of the Good Samaritan is the story of the Native Americans. We, like the man in the story, have fallen into the hands of thieves. We have suffered for centuries with the loss of our lands, languages and cultures, and have been left by our aggressors by the roadside, waiting to die."

I was somewhat taken back by his statement, and it too, burned in my soul. It illustrated to me just how painful the past still is among not only Native people in general, but even among strong Native Christian leaders and elders as well.

It must be made clear that his account of the previous night's wrestling match with God were not spoken with words of militant anger, but of somber reflection that our people have suffered much in the past five centuries.

The taking of our lands, language, culture and identity as Native people of North America was historically done in the name of Christ, by the arriving European immigrants, many of them the very people that represented Christ.

Within the growing movement of "Reconciliation" across the North American Christian landscape are various reconciliation "events." What is being done in these reconciliation events is Anglo American Christians are meeting with Native North Americans, and often falling down before them, asking for forgiveness for the sins of their ancestors. The mistreatment of Native North Americans in the past is the main focus of these events.

What seems to be overlooked in this movement is that there are truly two sides to this issue. What are the implications of this movement, and what does this issue of reconciliation look like from the "other side?"

It cannot be denied that, at its roots, racial reconciliation truly is a spiritual movement. Biblically, we as ministers of the gospel are charged with "the ministry of reconciliation."

As a Native Noth American, I must admit that I often find myself standing on the "other side" of this issue, and seriously trying to reconcile the biblical mandate with the pain and difficulty of being a part of a people group who have been seriously victimized over the past five centuries.

To illustrate my point, let me share with you the story of Simon Wiesenthal, known to many as one of the most outspoken analysts of the Holocaust, trying to keep history from ever repeating all that happened under the Nazis.

Wiesenthal's book is called *The Sunflower*, in which he shares a most dramatic and provocative experience, in which it is impossible to remain neutral.

He shares that, as a boy, he watched as the Nazis came into his home and took his own mother away, eventually taking her to a death camp where she died at the hands of those murderous people. He was to see his own grandmother shot in the stairway of her own home. When he had finally tallied all the members of his family who were brutally murdered by the Nazis, he counted 89 of them.

He later found himself to be in a concentration camp as well. All of a sudden, one day he found himself in a situation that haunted him for years.

A woman came and asked, "Excuse me, are you a Jew?" to which he replied, "Yes, I am."   She said, "There's a gentleman, a senior Nazi officer, dying in one of the hospital rooms here. He is asking to speak to a Jew. Would you be willing to come and meet with him?"

Wiesenthal did not know what it was about. He made his way to the room, saw a man lying in bed, bandaged from head to toe. The only openings in the bandages were at his nostrils, allowing him to breath, at his mouth, so he could mumble a few words, and at his ears, so he could hear sounds.

He leaned over towards Wiesenthal, and asked, "Sir, are you a Jew, are you telling me the truth?"

"Yes, I am," Wiesenthal replied.

"Give me your name," and he gave him his name.

He said, "Mr. Wiesenthal, I am dying. I am moments away from the end of my life. But I am not able to shake off this tormenting guilt that just won't go away. It is gnawing away at me. I have killed thousands of your people, as a matter of fact, the last thing I did was to torch a building with 300 Jews in it. I saw men, women and children screaming to be rescued. I saw babies being thrown out the window. I saw 300 of them die because of my order. And I did it to avenge some silly thing that we had been victimized with..."

"I cannot die without hearing someone from the Jewish race stand before me and say to me, 'I forgive you.' Would you please find it in your heart to stand before me and say those words, 'I forgive you?'"

Several times through this talk, Weisenthal recalls, he turned to walk away from this man. He could not bring himself to even listen to this man, but this man would keep beckoning and saying, "Please, please, do not go away..."

Finally, he said, "Would you, sir, would you please tell me you forgive me?"

Wiesenthal said, "I paused for 30 to 45 agonizing seconds, I could not bring myself to utter those words. I walked away, slamming the door shut."

For years Wiesenthal kept thinking about that incident, as it stayed on his mind.

Having it on his conscience, he wrote to thirty-two people worldwide. He wrote to some of the finest minds he knew, sociologists, theologians, and even Nobel laureates.

"I wrote to thirty-two, and simply asked this question, 'Do you think I did the right thing?'"

"Twenty-six wrote back and said, 'Absolutely!'"

"Six of them answered, 'They didn't think so, or were not sure.'"

Using this story as an illustration in his message to the del-

egates of the North American Congress for Itinerate Evange-
lists in 1994, noted evangelist and apologist Dr. Ravi Zacharias
commented, "I do not want to stand before you and pretend it
would be an easy thing for Wiesenthal to extend forgiveness. In
fact, this issue is larger than whether or not Wiesenthal did the
right thing. The larger issue is did he even have the prerogative
to do it on behalf of six million of his people that were led to
the slaughter."

Dr. Zacharias said about this illustration, "I only use this illustration to put into perspective to try and help you come to
grips with the agony of a nation that had been victimized, and
how easy forgiveness can suddenly seem, if you are in charge of
just saying, 'Will you forgive my people?'"

I believe this articulates better than any words that I could
write, the wrestling match I personally find myself in at times,
when it comes to the issue of racial reconciliation. This is my
core struggle. I cannot say that I speak for all Native ministers,
and would not assume to do so. I can only say that these are my
burdens, even after walking with the Lord for over twenty-four
years, and being a third generation Native Christian.

Reconciliation is not an easy thing to deal with, especially for
those who suffer the agony of a nation that has been victimized.
In direct contrast with the statement already made, "as easy forgiveness can suddenly seem, if you are in charge of just saying,
'Will you forgive my people," is the other side, and that is, "how
difficult forgiveness can seem if you are a part of the people
who have been the victims."

To put it in as clear a picture as I can, applying it to me personally, racial reconciliation is at best difficult for a victimized
people, and at worst, impossible to come to terms with by victimized people, without divine intervention. Even then, the
choice is not easy, for if we extend forgiveness and seek reconciliation today, the challenge is to keep a remembering mind tomorrow from not reliving the pain of past history tomorrow.
This is the challenge of the oppressed.

In this very painful area, the Native North American and the

Jew have much in common. For the Jew, the struggle of dealing with the suffering of the Holocaust and genocide has its parallel with the Native North American and our not so distant past experience of genocide. The commonality is drastically evident in these two highly similar people groups. History, in fact, has not adequately explained the horrors in North America, especially in comparison to the horrors of the Holocaust.

None can dispute the gruesome end results of the Holocaust. Well over six million Jews lost their lives at the hands of Hitler's regime. The pain still lingers for countless numbers of Jews as they look to this painful part of their past.

But what about the Native Americans? How does our history compare to their experience? As I have already noted, before the European migration to this land, there were anywhere from eight to twelve million aboriginal people covering the landscape of North America. By the turn of the twentieth century, however, that population had dwindled down to just over two hundred thousand! Can you see the enormity of the genocide Native America has faced? While over six million Jews were slaughtered in the holocaust, at least half again to almost double that amount of my people died through the very same process! I raise this point not in any way to diminish the ravages of what the Jews endured, but to point out, in comparison, the tragedy of the Native American experience, and the world's comparative lack of response to this blatant genocide that is to me a serious blot on not only our nation, but the Church of Jesus Christ, who implicitly shared in this process.

It is very difficult for me to see how the leaders of our nation are going to rise to this occasion and make right the past wrongs any time soon. In fact, even if they tried, their attempts would fall short, for true reconciliation and true repentance cannot happen from that perspective. It is first and foremost an issue of the heart. That is why, I believe, the Body of Christ plays the key role in fostering repentance and reconciliation. There is no other place for repentance to take place, but at the foot of Calvary's cross.

The only hope for true reconciliation can only be found through Christ, because He is the only One that can heal a wounded heart, and wounded memories. True reconciliation can only be found at the foot of the cross, and only through the atoning work of Christ. He is the answer for the hurt of the Jew, and He is the answer for the hurt of the Native American.

Dr. Zacharias touched also on what, to me, is a core issue when it comes to racial reconciliation. That is the issue of prerogative.

Do I, as a Native American living in this day and age, have the prerogative to extend forgiveness to an individual of another race, who represents a people who have played the role of the "thieves in the Good Samaritan parable," as it relates to Native Americans? I personally struggle with this issue.

The concerns I have are these:

First, can I assume the privilege of representing complete nations and peoples without that privilege being granted me by the same?

It seems to me that to assume this authority is to step beyond the level of reason. I have seen in previous "reconciliation events" involving Native Americans where Anglo Christians fall at the feet of Native people, repenting for the sins of their ancestors, and asking the Native people forgiveness on behalf of their ancestors.

I personally struggle with this. Of the two parties, it is easier for those on the Anglo side to go through this process, but much more difficult for the Native person. I believe it is assuming more responsibility than we as Native persons have been given by our own tribal leaders and authorities. What happens when Native traditionalists and militants find out that Native Christians are extending forgiveness in the name of Christ? What happens when they offer forgiveness to the descendants of homesteaders and pioneers whose movement westward came at the expense of the Native traditional way of life? In my opinion, this would only entrench Native traditionalists and militants in stronger defiance of Christ and Christianity, thus ending up causing more harm than help in making inroads to hardened Native hearts.

Secondly, what happens after a reconciliation event is concluded?

What happens in the mind of the one asking forgiveness once that forgiveness and reconciliation is extended?

In his mind, does he feel that now finally, he and his ancestors are completely absolved of any sense of responsibility for past atrocities, and everything is now forgiven and they can now get on with their lives? My fear is that now he will freely go on his way, unloaded of a sense of guilt for the past, living in the American mainstream, while those of us who have extended the forgiveness and responded to their plea for reconciliation still lie there on the roadside, with our clothing still gone, left half dead, while priests and Levites pass by on the other side, unwilling to get involved!

As I approach the issue of racial reconciliation, especially after hearing the exegesis (a scholarly explanation or interpretation of the Bible or Bible passage), and plea of my Native Christian elder on the Good Samaritan, I am compelled to share some thoughts to clarify our understanding of what biblical reconciliation really means to one from the "other side of the tracks."

First, reconciliation must be viewed from both sides.

It has often been those from dominant societies that initiate the call to reconciliation. Those from the dominant cultures need to understand that how they see reconciliation may not necessarily be how those from oppressed societies see this issue.

The issue of prerogative must be addressed, and settled before oppressed people can completely feel free to "represent" their ancestors in playing the role of "forgiver." If it truly is not our prerogative to stand representing our ancestors and fallen warriors, how do the implications of that affect racial reconciliation?

One thought I feel compelled to share in this regard, though, is this. After much soul searching, I personally feel that I cannot assume the role of "representative" of whole people groups, tribes and nations, present and past, unless that designation be given me by my people. The chances of that actually happening are next to nil!

How then do I approach the issue of racial reconciliation. The only reasonable answer left to me is that I can't do it corporately, but I can sure do it personally!

Scripture reminds me that if my brother has offended me I must go to him personally and initiate the process of confrontation and illumination, which in turn leads to repentance and reconciliation. I have to deal with the prejudices and ill will that I bear personally to those I know who have offended either me directly, or even to my people, corporately. Repentance and reconciliation then becomes intensely personal.

Second, we must teach that reconciliation is not the end, but the beginning.

As previously said, one of my greatest fears is that once reconciliation has occurred, what happens to the two parties involved? Does the offender go off, absolved, and get on with his life, while the offended is still lying on the roadside, beaten, naked and left for dead?

We are reminded in Acts 26:20, "I preached that they should repent, and turn to God, and prove their repentance by their deeds."

Scripture is clear in its admonition to offenders who repent. Prove your repentance by your deeds! Get involved! From the side of the man lying in the road, the greatest thing that anybody could do would be to change their agenda and get involved in meeting the need of the moment. Get involved with a motivation that is based on the potential and not the plight of our people.

As that applies to Native Americans, what are the real felt needs of Native people? What are the things, practically, that need to be done to show that true racial reconciliation is beginning? To Native Americans, of utmost importance is the deeds that confirm the repentance, more so than repentance itself.

What are some of the deeds that need to be evident for Native people to embrace reconciliation? I think that first, there needs to be a greater sense of accountability for the distribution of the gospel in America. What a shame that after centuries of living in a "gospel rich land," with churches on almost every corner of our communities, that the vast number of Native Americans are still unevangelized.

Of the fifty one million aboriginal people found in over twelve hundred tribes today in the Western Hemisphere, over five hundred tribes are yet to be reached with the gospel!

There is a greater need for more workers, finances, and prayer to be invested in organizations and denominations that are willing to minister with a culturally sensitive approach to administration and philosophy of ministry among Native Americans.

Individuals and churches should be encouraged to get solidly behind ministry organizations that are Native led, for it is these organizations that will be most effective among Native people, and will have the respect and endorsement of Native people.

We have reached a time in Native ministries where there are a growing number of qualified Native leaders emerging, who need the encouragement and support of the Body of Christ in general. God is giving us new dreams and visions about developing effective ministry among our people, but it will take partnerships in turning our dreams into reality.

Another key practical element in the process of racial reconciliation is to challenge multi-cultural denominations and organizations to open the doors of leadership, even at the highest levels, to those from outside the Anglo community. This is definitely one of the most blatant mistakes modern Christianity continues to make. It involves the majority of denominations and mission organizations that are multi-cultural in their outreach.

But, just like reconciliation is two-sided, the need to change mindsets and mentalities is also two sided. I would like to encourage a turnaround of mentality among our Native Christians as well. For centuries, we have been on the receiving end of missionary endeavors. The time has come for us to move from being the recipients of missions, to that of participants in mis-

sions. Some of my recent international ministry has opened my
eyes to the tremendous "advantage" Native aboriginal missionaries would have in many countries. Native missionaries would
compliment and bring new perspectives to world evangelization
alongside the traditional "American missionary."

I live for the day when we will be sending, from Native
churches, qualified, Spirit-filled Native missionaries to the uttermost part of the earth! That is my life's goal, and to which my
entire energies are committed.

I take encouragement because, as the world, and even the
Body of Christ, looks at Native Americans, we are looked upon
as "down and out," and "underdogs." That encourages me, because as I have studied the Bible, I have learned the lesson of
God and underdogs.

A change in mindsets and mentalities among both the dominant society and the minority church would bring about one of
the most revolutionary moves of God's Holy Spirit in our day.
The end result would be greater love for one another, greater
unity, and fulfillment of Christ's Great Commission, and a has-
tening of bringing back the King!

1   Alvin M. Josephy, Jr. *Now That The Buffalo's Gone*, Alfred A. Knopf, Page 31.

2   Ibid. Pages 77-78.

3   *Report of the Committee on Racial Reconciliation and Social Justice*, 1997 General
     Council, The Christian and Missionary Alliance.

Chapter 4

Christianity
and
Today's Indian

ONE OF THE BASIC FACTS about ministry among Native American people is that it has been done historically, and even to this day, primarily by the Anglo American church, and Anglo American missionaries. Rarely have we seen any other model for ministry in the history of Indian work.

Not too many other cultural groups have worked among Native people, but I sense that this could well change in the days to come. There is a seemingly growing interest among other cultural groups (such as Koreans, Chinese, Hispanics, etc.) to work among Native Americans. New alliances are being formed between church bodies of various international communities and Native ministry organizations here in North America. We can be sure of the fact that, in the future there are going to be more and more workers from a diversity of cultural and ethnic backgrounds spread across Native America involved in cross-cultural evangelism and church planting.

Along with those, primarily Anglo cross-cultural workers, there have been a number of Native converts who have sensed the call of God on their lives and have pursued the ministry. This has usually been done on a local level, as a pastor, often under the guidance and mentoring of a missionary.

Ministry to the Native people of North America is quite widespread, from all the way up into the frozen Arctic among the Eskimos, to the Seminoles of the Everglades in Florida.

Administration of Native ministries in America and Canada fall basically under two different systems.

In Canada, much of the missionary activity is carried out by independent, nondenominational organizations. Once churches are established by such mission groups, they then can affiliate with a Native ecclesiastical body, such as the Native Evangelical Fellowship of Canada. Then the administration of these Native churches are Native led through a national Native church.

In America, we also have a great number of independent mission organizations, whose ministries extend across our land. Most of these mission groups are smaller, with only a handful of local operations established and ongoing.

What we do have in America however, which is different from Canada, is a stronger denominationally based outreach. The reason we have a stronger denominational ministry in America is because of the assigning of denominations by the government to the various tribes back in the 1800s.

If you view success numerically, only a few denominations would be considered successful. The Southern Baptists have more than six hundred Native churches nationwide, with about two hundred in Oklahoma alone, and the Assemblies of God have close to two hundred churches and several Native Bible Colleges across the country. Methodists are also quite strong in some areas of the country.

But for the most part, most denominations, after decades of ministry, have very few Native churches. Most of them are small, struggling works.

The challenge, I believe, in modern Native ministry, is basically twofold.

First, we have to realize that for Native Americans, the past never dies. Dealing with and overcoming the past mistakes and even atrocities committed against Native people during the development and expansion of the American society and the planting of the Church in North America is a major challenge, and one that must not be brushed aside or avoided by the Body of Christ. This issue is of utmost importance! We have already dealt, to some extent in the previous chapter about this challenge, so I want to focus in on what I see as the other significant challenge we face today.

That second challenge is the struggle Native people have in relating to, and working on an equal basis in, denominations and organizations that even to this day are controlled, led and administered by leadership that is almost exclusively from the dominant society.

The end result of the dynamic of such led groups is often a continuation of traditional and often outdated and ineffective methodologies that are from a non-Native mind set and world view.

In a later chapter, I want to present to you what I believe is a biblical model for Native churches, that I believe will help change this. But first, let me explain why I believe that not only has the church historically missed the mark in its outreach to our people, but continues to walk down a path that will ensure limited success among Native Americans.

As we look today at the vast number of denominations working among Native Americans, one thing becomes vividly clear.

Though many consider themselves as all inclusive organizations, embracing and desiring all cultures to be included, the leadership, power and control continue to be almost exclusively Anglo-American. This is not only the way it is, but the dynamic of this system has tremendous implications for Native American ministry.

Of course there are also a number of "ethnic" denominations, particularly in the Black community, that are set up and administered from within their own community. But none of these denominations, at least to my understanding, minister among Native people, or if they do, it is on a very limited basis.

The bottom line, because of this dynamic, is that Native

Americans continue to look at the gospel of Jesus Christ as the Whiteman's Gospel because, in America, it sure has that look.

It would be interesting to do a survey of all the major denominational headquarters and ask one simple question. How many non-Anglo people do you have serving in leadership within your organization?

My observation has been that even though denominations will often hire a Native person, or others from other minority groups to serve as a representative of their people, and even give that person an impressive title, the denominational structure insures that the real power and authority and decision making will continue to be kept in the Anglo led hierarchy. Where there are structures in place to eventually bring Native ministry to an equal footing with others within the organization, the membership and income needed to have equal status is hard to acquire, especially among such a hardened and resistant people group as Native Americans.

There are other discrepancies that are faced within denominations that need to be addressed. Often has been the case when the pay scale has been different in denominational leadership, depending on whether or not the person is white or Indian, even if the job description was the same. Denominations have begun to address this inequity, but only after it began to be made known to their constituencies that this inequality truly did exist.

I don't think the leadership in denominations is really fully aware of just how important these issues are to the various cultural groups that it works among. Let me share with you some examples I am aware of to help illustrate this point.

There was a Native leader within a denomination who was elected to direct the Native ministries of that denomination. This person had to go through an orientation program at their national office.

A part of that orientation was to spend some time with different national leaders in the division that the Indian work was under. Just prior to his election, the national office had hired to one of the top national office positions, an ethnic leader, who was one of the first to break through the "color barrier" of their national leadership. Along with meeting other leaders in the division, he spent some time with this man, just before he was going to go to lunch with another Anglo leader.

Having this visit with the ethnic leader fresh in his mind, he commented to the Anglo taking him to lunch, "It sure is good to see some color here at the national office!"

This particular Anglo leader happened to have as his secretary, another "person of color." There were several "ethnic" people working at the office, all of whom, except the ethnic leader previously mentioned, were in clerical positions.

His lunch companion responded, "Well, brother, we try to hire secretarial help from all races. It's not easy, but we are working at it!"

The Native leader laughed and cried inside, realizing that he and the Anglo leader were on two completely different wave lengths. The one automatically thought in terms of the "help," while the Native leader was thinking in terms of "leadership roles" within the organization.

Sometimes there are leadership meetings where discussions have included issues relating to paternalism. Included in one forum was a rehearsal of how Anglo paternalism positively affects minority people who were, in the eyes of Anglo leadership, not yet capable of leadership.

I can recall once when I was church planting and pastoring a Native church in Phoenix, Arizona, our family was asked to sing and speak at a conference of another denomination's Native ministries. It happened to be in Phoenix, so we were delighted to go, since it was right in our own community.

After singing, I spoke for a few minutes on my vision and burden to encourage Native people to see beyond themselves, and get involved in reaching the world for Christ. I can still see the response of those Native pastors as they were seeing, some for the very first time, that we must move beyond our limited view of ministry to just our people, to that of being world Christians.

I will never forget, after I shared those thoughts, their denominational director of their ethnic ministries in America, who
was a white man, got up after me to give a few comments. His
words ring in my ears to this day.

He said, "Brother Smith, I appreciate what you had to say,
about Indian people going as missionaries to the world, but it
just can't be done! There are too many Native people who are
yet to be reached, so Native people should concentrate on just
their own people. Leave world missions up to us (meaning the
Anglo Church)."

My heart sank as I heard these words. You see, all is not well
in the Body of Christ when we have people in positions of power,
influence and leadership, that continue to promote the message
that the gospel is the "Whiteman's Gospel." It brings to mind
the strongly indicting words of Vine Deloria,

> *No other field of endeavor in America today has as much
> blatant racial discrimination as does the field of Christian missions
> to the American Indian people. It is a marvel that so many Indian
> people still want to do work for the churches.[1]*

I think these illustrations are a fair representation of the challenge that the Anglo American Christian leader faces when it
comes to ingrained views of people from other races. Again,
please realize that I share these illustrations not to condemn, but
to bring to light some real issues facing the Body of Christ, that
if not corrected, will insure less than the most effective and successful ministries in our denominational works. That's really the
bottom line! If these don't suffice, I could share many more
with you that would lend support to the difficulty dominant societies have when it comes to feeling that others of other cultures are not automatically considered capable and qualified to
assume roles of leadership, and should be treated on an equal
basis with those from their own society.

In the over twenty-five years I have been in ministry, I have
visited hundreds, if not thousands, of Anglo churches. Those
many visits into non-Indian settings have confirmed to me just
how some in the dominant society, and in particular the Chris-

tian community, all too often view themselves, as well as Native people.

It must be said that by and large, the Christian community in the dominant society, including church leadership, approaches people of other backgrounds with a sincere and genuine heart. To me, the sincerity of most is genuine, but how that sincerity of heart becomes translated into action often leaves much to be desired. All too often the heart is open, but the mind is closed.

There is an ingrained mindset that needs to be recognized and refined through the power of the Holy Spirit. For the most part, those in the Body of Christ, from positions of leadership on down to the laity, don't even realize how narrow their focus can be when it comes to people of other cultures. The irony of this is that we take great pride in reaching all cultures through active missionary involvement!

Perhaps it is important for the denominational leaders in power today to have these things, which are personally painful for me to speak about, brought out for their serious consideration. For what is in the heart of leadership, whether it is good or bad, has to filter down to the constituencies they represent. If this type of attitude is prevalent in the hallowed halls of our ecclesiastical leaders, it will be evident all the way down even to the local church.

What Is Our Motivation For Ministry?

Realizing that the bulk of denominational ministry is led and directed from the perspective of a dominant society, how does that affect the motive or motivation for ministry?

Or perhaps this issue would be better looked at if we would ask the question, "What importance does our motivation have in relation to our ministry?"

I would have to say that motivation is one of the most important elements in ministry, affecting everything we do, how our ministry is carried out, and to what extent we will be effective in it. I can't overemphasize the importance of motivation for ministry.

Given the fact that the bulk of ministry among Native Americans is conducted from a cross-cultural perspective, and that being from the dominant society to the Indian culture, it is important for non-Indian people working among our people to examine their motivation for ministry. This one factor, I believe, is critical, because ultimately, motives shape methodologies.

As I see it, we can basically define motivation for Native ministry in two distinct categories. Workers among our people are out there doing their ministry because of either a motivation that is based on the perception of our Plight or Problems, or they are there because of a motivation that is based on the perception of our Potential.

A look back historically shows that the vast majority of mission agencies and organizations ministering among our people were and are there because they were motivated by the plight or problems facing Native Americans. I say vast majority, but I am also mindful of the fact that some of the greatest missionaries in the history of the church spent either some or all of their lives among our people, and the fruit of their ministry have lasted to this day. I do want to say more about them later.

In my opinion, though, today there are many who are ministering to Native Americans who have never really considered what truly has motivated them to enter Native ministry. Can we truly say we are motivated by the potential our people possess, as underdogs, to do great things for God? Or have we entered the work based upon a condescending perception of the plight of the Native Americans?

The proof of what your motivation is will be evident by the way you conduct your ministry.

A plight-based ministry is a self perpetuating kind of ministry, and is the easiest one to present to the supporters of that mission work. It is the kind that any worker will be able to sustain for a whole career, as long as those supporting churches continue to hear about the plight of the Native Americans.

A plight-based ministry meets a tremendous need for supporting churches, because it provides a means by which they can help those who are less fortunate, which is a biblical command, but in doing so often perpetuates the stereotypical view that those from the dominant society churches have of Native Americans. It also opens up avenues of ministry for dominant society churches that, again help them fulfill their biblical mandate. However, in doing so, they actually hinder and impede the very people their ministry is intended to help.

I believe that ultimately, plight-based ministry and the ensuing failure of the church to entrust leadership, etc., in Native people is ultimately an issue of faith, or lack of it, not in man, but rather in God. It is God who makes it possible for anyone, from any culture, to walk in His ways. So when there are those who feel that they can't trust the Native people to lead the church are really saying that they lack confidence in the Lord, Himself, to build His church among Native people.

Let me explain.

We are all well aware that throughout the years of missionary efforts among Native Americans, Anglo churches have been not only the providers of the financial resources to enable the missionaries to go, but they have been the ones to raise the money for and the work crews to build the churches, schools, etc., of most mission stations across Indian America. Along with financial resources, materials, and work crews, we can't fail to mention the "mission boxes" and "used clothing" boxes that continue to fill many of the 18 wheelers crisscrossing America today.

While it meets the need of the supporting church, have we ever stopped to think about the impact these good deeds have on those it is intended to help?

There is an automatic perception formed by dominant society Christians that since I am doing this out of my concern and good heart, that the natural response and impact it will have on those I am directing this to will be positive, and it will help them. But that isn't always the case.

When any missionary minded church, which is motivated by the plight or the problem of Native Americans, responds to a need based on the plight or problem, it is ensuring that the plight or problems will continue to be perpetuated.

When any missionary minded church raises money for a building project on some Indian mission station, and then sends a work crew out to build the structure, the end result is that the Native people in that community will never have a sense of ownership, nor will they take the responsibility of maintaining it since it's not theirs.

It reminds me of an incident that happened to an Anglo pastor friend of mine, back in the early 1970s, who pastors a great church in southern California. He asked one of our Navajo pastors when his church could come out and paint the Navajo's church.

The Navajo pastor matter of factly responded, "We don't go and paint your church, so why should you come and paint ours? That's our responsibility, to take care of our own facilities!"

Even to this day, when I see this pastor, he reminds me of that eye opening experience which changed his outlook on how the church should engage in the ministry of helps.

The used clothing boxes that have filled mission station after mission station is another example of a project that on the one side helps meet the biblical mandate of the dominant society churches, but in many ways proves to be counterproductive to the people it is intended to serve, and is definitely a plight motivated form of help. And oh, what some of those boxes contain!

I remember my wife sharing that once when they were at Navajo Mountain, the church received a mission box filled with spiked high heel shoes, but only the left side. Another box came that was filled with strapless ballroom formal dresses. I could just imagine those dear Navajo women, out there in the high desert all day long, herding their sheep hobbling around with one spiked high heel shoe and the other barefoot, and twirling around the sheep corral in their strapless evening gowns! And yes, they even suffered from the ultimate humiliation, when they actually did receive a box full of, you guessed it, the proverbial used tea bags.

What does it say to a Native person, when boxes of someone

else's discarded items are sent to them? It says to the Indian's mind, "These items are no longer of use to the white man, so now he will send them to the Indians. He doesn't want them, nor need them, but surely we will."

It continues to perpetuate in Native people's minds their low self image, and does nothing to help build their self esteem. Plight motivated ministry unwittingly continues to perpetuate just such mentalities.

Now there are truly those who are in need, within the Indian cultures, as well as any other culture here in America. The streets of our communities are filled with the homeless, the destitute, and the outcasts from all cultural backgrounds, and we all must respond to those in need. But even there, if our motive for ministry is based on the plight or the problem, we will establish ministries that will meet the plight or the problem, but will not provide the means by which those in despair can move beyond the present into a better future.

Remember the great line "Give a man a fish, and you feed him for a day. Teach a man to fish and you feed him for a lifetime?" How true that statement is. That statement basically defines the difference between the two motivations. That is why motivation for ministry, to even the ones in greatest need should be based on the potential, and not on the plight.

I think it is important to realize that biblical compassion must be the primary motivation for any cross-cultural ministry, but compassion must not lead to condescension. Having a heart for a people is biblical, keeping them as perpetual receivers is not.

The goal of developing strong, Native churches, which move from the receiving end to the participating end of ministry will never be done through plight-based missions. If that is what we truly want to see among Native Americans, then a shift in the motivation of missionaries and even Native pastors must happen, and happen soon. Otherwise, we will lose another generation of our people due to the irrelevancy of plight motivated methods.

Ministry that is motivated by the potential, and not the plight

has rarely been seen here in America among Native Americans, and
that has contributed to the reason Native people have not bought
stock in the message of Christianity. It brings to mind a few other
statements by Vine Deloria, Jr.,

> *The impotency and irrelevancy of the Christian message has meant
> a return to traditional religion by Indian people.*
>
> *The determination of white churches to keep Indian congregations
> in a mission status is their greatest sin. But it is more a sin against
> themselves than it is against Indian people. For the national churches
> do not realize how obsolete their conceptions have become and they
> continue to tread the same path they walked centuries ago.*
>
> *Many Indians believe that the Indian gods will return when the
> Indian people throw out the white man's religion and return to the
> ways of their fathers. Whether or not this thinking is realistic is not
> the question. Rather, the question is one of response and responsibil-
> ity of the missionaries today. Will they continue to be a burden or
> not? Can the white man's religion make one final effort to be real, or
> must it too vanish like its predecessors from the old world?* [2]

The dilemma, however, is that for the most part, the church
and its leaders do not see that how they have come across to
Native Americans and to other cultural groups has provided the
ammunition that fuels just such thoughts of Christianity's irrelevancy.

How then are we to change? How should the Body of Christ,
from the top down, evaluate how it structurally keeps the power,
control and influence within primarily one cultural group, and
thus alienates at least the Native American, and probably many
other minority branches of its constituencies?

How should local churches evaluate their own motivations
for their missionary involvement?

Let me speak to the first question.

I think we need to evaluate all aspects of Native ministry in
every denomination and independent mission society working
among us. We also need to evaluate mission principles that we
have promoted and utilized without evaluating whether or not
they are appropriate for our distinct ministry.

As an example, most workers in Native ministry adhere to and promote loudly the need to operate with the "Indigenous Principles" as our guide. The indigenous principles incorporate three guidelines that have been taught to us by the missionaries and that most Native ministries have set out as goals to attain. These three pillars are to become:

1. Self-Supporting
2. Self-Governing
3. Self-Propagating

It all sounds good and right, but have we ever asked ourselves if these principles are biblical principles, or are they primarily cultural principles? They definitely have been the principles that have been promoted for years as the ideal for Native ministry, but let me ask you this question—is it biblical?

A look into Scripture shows not self-sufficiency, but rather inter-dependency among Jewish and Gentile churches. In fact, several occasions stand out in my mind, and this is crucial, where the parent Jewish church, was the recipient of gifts, offerings, and blessings from the daughter Gentile churches! That is illustrated by the church in Antioch in Acts 11, and the Macedonian church in Romans 15. This inter-dependency was not a one way street, and exclusively from the parent to the child, but often from the child back to the parent. It was evident that every established work, regardless what culture it was from, was responsible to have a vision for the lost of all cultures, and for blessing the believers from other cultural churches if they were to experience the blessing of God.

As we will see in the following chapter, the church was at its best when there was a plurality of leadership present that was truly representative of the diversity of the whole. The concept of self-governing implies that "self" is limited to a specific cultural or racial group, and nobody outside that group need apply. But that's not biblical! That's why I believe so strongly that the Body of Christ, especially in North America is selling itself short, and missing God's mark, when leadership is, for the most part, exclusively from only one of the cultures, the dominant society, that makes up the cultural diversity of the constituency it represents.

Also, the issue of self-propagation again implies that "self" limits involvement to only those from within the culture represented. There is a perception that you are only able to be successful when your vision and your work are limited to the context of your own culture. In other words, the homogeneous concept where each cultural group works among only their own and from their own fits this principle well, but it's hard to see this principle endorsed in Scripture. To the contrary, Scripture challenges the whole of Christ's Church to be a witness to all nations. Native Americans must assume our responsibility for the world. The Chinese must assume their responsibility for the world. The Haitians, the Cambodians, the Vietnamese, the Russians the Mongolians and every—panta ta ethne—nation that has been touched by the gospel all must move from being a recipient to that of an active participant in fulfilling the Great Commission if we are to be the Church Christ envisions for these end times.

If the indigenous principles, as commonly defined, are not biblical principles, then we must ask ourselves if they are cultural principles. I think this is a more accurate category to place these principles in, especially as we see this concept played out in North America.

What is the measuring rod used by the American church to evaluate success in ministry? The three standards of success are clearly Size, Sufficiency and Scope, or the three pillars of indigenous principles. Success in America is always based on how large a congregation you have. Attend any national church conference and the talk over coffee among clergy will always center on how large a church you pastor, or how many members you now have. Another measuring rod of success in the American church is how large of a budget do you operate with, and how many "tithing units" (whatever that means!) your church has, and how much money you give to support missions (regardless of whether or not you are culturally sensitive to the multiplicity of cultures within a few mile radius of the church).

To be successful in the American church you have to become self-supporting, self-governing, and self-propagating. Since the American church has led the way in missionary activity, its missionary program has adopted the same evaluation of success in missions as the sending American church has used to evaluate its own success, all the while promoting these principles as "biblical principles."

The question, then, that must be asked is, "are we promoting a form of evaluation of success in mission work that is not biblical, and may actually be leading us down a road that keeps cultural walls of partition in place?" The further question that needs to be considered, then, is this. "Does the American church have a measuring rod of success that is at its worst, not biblical, and at its best primarily cultural, based upon the American secular view of success?"

I would encourage the Native church to have as its standard of evaluation of success the principles attributed to Jesus Christ, where in Isaiah 61:1-3 it says of Him,

> *The Spirit of the Sovereign Lord is on me, because the Lord has anointed me to preach good news to the poor. He has sent me to bind up the brokenhearted, to proclaim freedom for the captives and release from darkness for the prisoners, to proclaim the year of the Lord's favor and the day of vengeance of our God, to comfort all who mourn, and provide for those who grieve in Zion—to bestow on them a crown of beauty instead of ashes, the oil of gladness instead of mourning, and a garment of praise instead of a spirit of despair. They will be called oaks of righteousness, a planting of the Lord for the display of His splendor.*

Keep in mind the principle of God and underdogs. As radical as this might sound, we need to be reminded that God has not typically and historically used the dominant societies of this world to do His greatest work through, but He delights to use underdogs. If Isaiah 61 is truly a biblical principle and measuring rod of success, then the Body of Christ would have to ac-

knowledge that the Native church is meeting that high standard
of success. Brother, that encourages me more than wanting to
see the first Native mega-church established, with the priority
being how many came out last Sunday morning!

I do realize, however, that God has used the American church,
truly a dominant society church, to the degree He has. It is wonderful to see, and I wouldn't be serving Christ had it not been
for the faithfulness of the American church. But I must reiterate
that the challenge for the American church lies in the biblically
based realization that the mighty, noble, and influential have a
greater tendency to lean on and use as a measuring rod of success, their own abilities, resources and power to accomplish things
in the spiritual world that can never be done, to their greatest
level of impact, by those human powers.

Just think, then, of how much more effective the Body of
Christ would be when the underdogs are included in providing
the leadership, influence, motivation and ideas from his or her
own perspective and world view!

It reminds me of a story a Mohawk colleague in ministry
shared with me once. He was approached by a non-Indian who,
when he came face to face with this Mohawk, raised his hand
and said, "How!"

My Mohawk friend's response to this intelligent man's greet-
ing was this. "Sir, we know how, all we need now is a chance!"

How should denominations that are engaged in ministry to
Native Americans best structure this branch of ministry to be
most effective?

I think there are two tracks that must be considered, the first
being probably the most palatable to denominational leadership,
as it simply involves some changes within.

The second track I would propose, I'm sure will be viewed by
those who rule as probably too radical a change for denominations, which are so protective of their "turf," to consider at this
stage of the game. Whichever track is best, I would remind us
that either option must be based on a biblical view of interde-
pendency, and not self based.

Let me share with you these two tracks, and let the chips fall where they may. If I wasn't viewed as radical before, I'm sure I will be now!

The first track involves a keeping of Native ministries within the various denominations, but major philosophical changes need to be implemented if we are serious about developing strong Native denominationally affiliated churches.

Native ministry in and of itself is very difficult, even if the best and most appropriate structure were in place. We face major obstacles in reaching Native Americans with the gospel, but the challenge is made even greater when denominations fail to provide a climate in which Native church growth can occur. I believe the key to developing a climate by which Native ministry will be most successful lies in a denomination's willingness to evaluate, and if necessary, relinquish its domineering and heavy hand of oversight of Native ministries, which is usually under the oversight of an Anglo national leader. As that happens, then turn true responsibility, with accountability, to a fully empowered Native leader who is not there in a token position, but is able to lead his people with the full endorsement and blessing of the denomination behind him.

I think there continues to exist, to varying degrees, concerns about entrusting to Native Americans the doctrines, polity and care of denominational ministry. I believe there is an unacknowledged fear that if the ministry of the denomination was truly turned over to Native people, we might not handle the leadership responsibilities up to the standard that has been carried out to this point, regardless of how ineffective the structure has been over the years. The potential of losing control of the power over minority people, no matter what arena we are dealing with, is probably one of the most difficult things for the dominant society to face, including the church. But in reality, hasn't the failure of decades and even centuries of ministry among Native Americans cry out for this kind of change?

There needs to be flexibility, as much as denominational polity and structure will allow, for a culturally sensitive-based structure for Native churches. I have been in some denominational Indian business meetings where most Indians attending think Roberts Rules of Order is the name of a Plains Indian Clergyman! Will denominations be flexible enough to allow a more culturally adapted style to its necessary business meetings? Or must we keep such a formalized structure that keeps our people feeling uncomfortable, and unable to relate?

I remember, for years we would have our annual meetings and do everything the way the missionaries taught us, even though we never quite understood much of parliamentary procedures. We went through years of considering items seriatim without even knowing what the Latin word seriatim even meant!

Now, denominations are not a bad thing, as some would like to make them to be, or as perhaps some might think I believe. I often hear of folk who think of denominations as ungodly, and not a true representation of the Church as it should be.

My thoughts are not that at all. Even though through this book, I share both the good and bad experiences those of us in denominational Native leadership have had within various denominational ministry, it shouldn't be construed that I am not committed to denominational ministry. I am! Believe me! Even as hard as some of my experiences have been, I love the message, the people and the "family" that comprise the denomination that I belong to.

There is definitely no denomination that is better than the next, for the greatest problem with Christianity is that it involves people, myself included! To me, what denominations provide in the positive sense really does outweigh the negatives.

What are some of the positives I see in denominations?

First, I think it does provide a sense of family. We all have the need to belong to a family unit, and family units do provide structure, protection, discipline and a sense of belonging that you don't find on your own.

It also provides you with a sense of direction, spiritual covering, and provides a channel to direct, what hopefully will be potential motivated help and ministry around the world.

In my twenty-five plus years of ministry, I have had the opportunity of visiting a number of foreign countries, many of which my denomination ministers in. There is just something that happens to you when you are in a far away land, when you see something that reminds you of home. For some, it may be the golden arches of a McDonalds Restaurant. For others, it may be as simple as holding a can of Coke in their hands. For me, I feel that I am really not as far away from home as I really am when I pull up to one of our churches or mission stations and see the good old familiar C&MA logo hanging from the door of a church or mission station.

Also, if we are to truly provide a climate in which Native churches can feel comfortable in a denominational structure, the issue of self-determination must be addressed.

We must have a sense that we are given the responsibility for the success or failure of our Native denominational ministry, and I believe we as Native leaders are willing to shoulder just that responsibility. The Native leaders, and not the centralized denominational leadership, must be entrusted with the responsibilities of budgeting and oversight of all resources for the work and personnel matters for both Indian and non-Indian workers, including even the placement and oversight of cross-cultural missionaries serving in its field.

The denomination that is willing to let the Native churches determine their own plans, procedures and priorities for growth, and bear the responsibility for such growth, is the one that will emerge from the pack as the leader of necessary change for Native American ministry.

On the other hand, the dominant society leadership has to be willing to allow such change, and give liberty for that to happen, and not see it as threatening to the purity of the denomination or its message. It will take great courage on the part of both the leadership and the Native churches to strive to meet those challenges. If denominations are willing to consciously work toward that end, the result will be very positive.

Native churches have to live in the balance of developing a

culturally sensitive form of polity and structure, and still feel an integral part of the denomination it finds itself in, if it is to succeed.

You will have Native churches that are operating within a framework with which they feel comfortable and which will be conducive for growth. They will also have a sense of appreciation for a denomination that is flexible enough to meet Native people in the framework of their world view and perspective. The natural outcome of such mind set will be a branch of a denomination that is committed to its message, for the methods are not overshadowing and disqualifying the message.

Not too long ago, denominational leadership from one denomination came out with a paper on "New Methodologies on Reaching Native Americans." When Native leaders made inquiry as to who developed this paper, and who was included in their research, they found out, much to their dismay, but not to their surprise, that this entire document was compiled without any Native person's involvement. It was written exclusively by Anglo leadership, and the people they contacted in their research for this document were all non-Indian leaders of other denominations and mission organizations. Not one single Native person was interviewed, nor were any Native person's views included in a powerful document that was going to provide the new and "more effective" philosophy of ministry that this denomination was to engage in as it worked among Native Americans! No wonder why Native people continue to feel that the gospel is the "Whiteman's Gospel!" Can we really blame them?

Another challenge I feel we need to face is the continual desire of some in denominational leadership to attempt to diminish the uniqueness of the Native American experience, and the church's past mistakes.

It seems to me that many denominations are not willing to see that Native Americans resist all efforts to minimize the drastic differences we have with the rest of the American society. Among recent immigrant people to North America, it seems that they have no problem with attempting to "melt" into the melting pot of the dominant American society. It is what they want to do. But for Native Americans, we are made of something that doesn't melt, and for us, just the opposite is true. We do reject anything that trivializes our heritage, and attempts to make us to feel like we are no different from the other people groups that we really and truthfully cannot relate to.

We have a unique heritage, including a history of past pain and suffering, done to our people at times even in the name of Christ, and we struggle to cope with those that attempt to gloss over those issues. In doing so, we feel trapped in a system that we cannot relate to or feel comfortable with. The burden is that in most denominations, Native ministry is not strong enough numerically or financially to have the leverage to invoke the kind of change necessary to provide a climate for Native church growth to happen. That's the dilemma Native Christian leaders all too often find themselves in as they work within the framework of denominational ministry.

If Native ministry remains as it presently is on this first track, I believe what would really help Native denominational churches, and the host of independent Native churches presently scattered across America, would be a national association of Native evangelical churches. This association would serve as a vehicle that would bring credibility and respect, on a national level, to the vast number of Native evangelical churches already in existence. It would provide a voice for Native evangelicals to be heard on an equal basis within ecclesiastical, governmental and even educational arenas nationwide.

The second track that I want to introduce in this book is the one that would meet, no doubt, with the strongest resistance from most denominational leaders, because it involves the creation of a National Native Christian denomination, similar to the Canadian model.

Before I develop this, let me say that I personally feel that if denominations and mission organizations would implement the changes mentioned in the first track, or some similar form of major restructuring, which would include a national Native association of evangelical churches, that would be the best route to take. There is however, great merit to the second track as well.

The Canadian model works well because of the stronger presence of independent organizations doing mission work. Once a mission work is established, it can choose to join the Native Evangelical Fellowship, which is Native led, and all ecclesiastical procedures including the licensing, ordination and oversight of Native pastors is done under the auspices of this nationwide Native "denomination."

It has been interesting to observe the growth and development of this model, which was started around 1970 by several strong Native Canadian leaders, including Dr. Tommy Francis, Rev. Bill Jackson, Rev. Stan Williams, Rev. Albert Tait, and Mr. Saul Keeash. These are all men that God used in a powerful way to establish a viable national Native fellowship.

Their growth as an organization has not been without its challenges, and even as recent as the past few years, they have had to deal with some difficult issues internally. They dealt with these issues in a way that provided both a learning experience, and a strengthening of this organization.

The challenge we face in America to see such a model develop lies in the multiplicity of denominations, and with such, a multiplicity of doctrinal stances and methodologies that are unique to each organization.

If this was to be a viable option to pursue, national denominations would need to be in agreement to such a drastic paradigm shift, and assist in the creation of such an ecclesiastical body. It could not be done without the blessing, cooperation and involvement of existing denominations willing to venture out into such uncharted waters. The rationale for denominations to undergo such a drastic shift, I think, is legitimate, and very, very simple. As previously stated, historically, denominations picked, chose, and were assigned by the government, the regions, reservations and tribes, much the same way children pick sides of a pickup baseball game at a local park. Denominations and their various doctrinal views were strongly entrenched into the fabric of local Native communities, and turf wars were an ongoing part of historical Native ministry.

In many ways, the isolationism and battling over doctrinal purity between organizations and denominations did much to demonstrate un-Christlike behavior among the churches, rather than modeling the unity of the Kingdom of God as described in Scripture.

What a statement the Body of Christ could make today, by admitting such wrongs of the past, and proving such repentance by deeds. That would include helping to establish, build, grow and enter into a partnership with a new, national Native evangelical denomination, where the centrality of Christ is preeminent, and reaching Native America and from there, the world is of primary importance!

This body, which would comprise Native churches from the denominations and even independent mission organizations that were willing to participate, would have to settle some major points of contention in its initial organizational process. Issues such as a Statement of Faith that would be inclusive enough to cover such diversity that would be represented by participating agencies would have to be settled on. Getting past that hurdle would be one of the most important step to forward such a vision. But I believe it can be done!

The major challenge one would face in this drastic paradigm shift would be to overcome the fear of denominational "turf" being infringed upon, and the continual denominational competition so prevalent in Indian country. A good example of denominational competition existed in Farmington, New Mexico, where in 1965 there were twenty-six denominations serving an estimated Navajo population of 250! It for just such a reason that denominations should at least be willing to consider developing such a partnership with a Native denomination. It would truly serve as a testimony of true biblical repentance and reconciliation over past mistakes and injustices so prevalent in historical Native ministry.

Dealing with the difficulty dominant society led ministries

have in relinquishing their power and control over cultural groups within their constituencies would also be a major obstacle, but again, if there is a willingness on the part of the Church to make such a step, what a tremendous statement the Church would be making to Native America!

This ecclesiastical body would elect its leadership from within. Its constituency would develop culturally sensitive policies and programs that would be born in the hearts and minds of Native people themselves.

By that, I mean an organizational structure that was informal enough to be acceptable to Native culture, and leadership that would reflect Native way of life. I would envision an administrative structure that would allow for spiritual oversight to be handled through a "Council of Elders," made up of key Native Christian elders from the participating agencies. The Body of Christ has hidden gems that have yet to be revealed to the larger Body in the Native Christian elders of North America.

The Body of Christ in America has many top named speakers, leaders and motivators, who are the ones visible at many major Christian events and gatherings. But when I think of some of our Native Christian elders, many of whom were faithful to their God without any kind of fanfare and public knowledge, often under trying and difficult experiences during the whole of their ministry careers, my heart fills!

You probably have never heard of some of these men, and I am even a bit hesitant to name them, for fear of leaving some of them out, but let me share them with you, just the same. These elders, many of whom have given their whole lives to Christian service among their people, may never get the honor due them in this life, but I know God has a special place of honor and reward for them when they finally make it home.

They are giants for Christ with names like Rev. Tom Claus, Rev. Kenneth Antone, Dr. Tommy Francis, Rev. Bill Jackson, Rev. Albert Tait, Rev. Stan Williams, Dr. Jerry Yellowhawk, Rev. Charles Lee, Rev. Herman Williams, Rev. Victor Kaneubbe, Rev. Andrew Maracle, Rev. Eddie Lindsay, Mr. Ray Smith, Rev. Art

Holmes, Mr. Wendle Tsoodle, Rev. Claudio Iglesias, Rev. Silas Correa, and on and on the list could go.

Elders such as these men would provide the spiritual oversight while others, perhaps younger leaders, would serve administratively in such a national Native ecclesiastical body.

This body would oversee the licensing, ordaining and oversight of the Native pastors and missionaries under its care, and would also serve the denominations as a conduit for all non-Indian missionaries desiring to go out through their denominational mission programs. It would be a cooperative venture, between an organization that would comprise Native American Christian leaders, and denominations and mission organizations engaged in Native ministry.

Funding for such an organization would come first and foremost from within the Native churches (this is imperative), and from the partnering denominations and mission organizations.

One of the things that concern me about the present day mentality of plight-based mission work among our people is that we are always presented as poor and in need of outside support to survive. Now it is true that many of our people live in poverty, but at the core of a Native person is a very generous and giving heart. The church has managed to, however, strip that generosity from us, as it operated in reservation after reservation with funds, personnel and all resources from the outside supporting churches. That again, is one of the negative results of plight motivated mission work.

You go to a powwow today, and you will see the generous heart of Native people in action. The traditional "giveaways" that I have observed have shown that our people do have a generous nature, and it only needs to be tapped by the body of Christ. The challenge we face in tapping that resource is that Native people will give only when they know it will help and benefit their people. Such an ecclesiastical structure would be viewed, no doubt, by Native people as very positive, and worthy of support.

I believe that if we give Native people a structure, whether that is within present denominational framework, or as a national Native ecclesiastical body, where they feel comfortable, there will be a generous spirit of giving to sustain the work from within as any other culture! The biblical principle of stewardship shows us that God blesses people, including Native Christians, when they support the work from within!

What would the role of the denominations be, after they turned the administration of their Native churches to such a new Native denominational body?

As previously mentioned, they would need to also invest financially in such a body, to help it develop and implement its projects and programs. I would envision the development of Native Sunday School curriculum, scholarships for Native students studying for the ministry, church planting strategies, global missions, and all other projects and programs most denominations have in existence for their constituencies. This would be accomplished, however, by and through Native people and from a Native perspective.

I also would envision the denominations placing missionary workers in locations only after consultation with, and under the recommendations of, this Native ecclesiastical body. What a contrast that would be from the ways of the past when they were assigned areas, without thought, by the U.S. and Canadian governments!

The options are unlimited, and many, I'm sure.

The other question raised deals with the local church. How should local churches evaluate their own motivations for their massive missionary involvement?

First of all, let me commend the American church for the very active involvement it has in reaching the world with the gospel of Christ. In many ways, their involvement in missions far surpasses many other parts of the Body of Christ worldwide.

But again the question does not imply a lack of involvement. The question I raise speaks to the motivation for their involvement in world evangelization.

Is the motivation for such deep involvement in reaching the world based on the perceived plight of people globally, or is it motivated by a mentality that sees beyond the present situation, and envisions those who are being reached by their efforts also taking on their responsibility as a full partner in world evangelization? Motivation will dictate methodologies, and this is where the difference lies.

A passage of Scripture that is relevant to this discussion, both for the dominant society and for the other parts of the body of Christ is Romans 11:1-25.

It's clear that the fellowship in Rome is expressly stated by Paul not to be of his own founding. It is the exception to Paul's rule not to build on another man's foundation. So the writing of this letter was a bit out of Paul's normal operating procedures.

Who started this church and how it started is uncertain. It is believed that the church in Rome was started by the witness and labors of Christians who were a part of the Roman Empire, in the habit of traveling to and from Rome.

By the time Paul wrote this letter, from Corinth around AD 55, he is writing to a large, multi-cultural church made up of both Jews and Gentiles, with the stronger number probably being Gentile.

He makes an interesting statement and develops an analogy that is worthy of our consideration.

In verse 11, he says,

Again I ask: Did they (the Jews) stumble so as to fall beyond recovery? Not at all! Rather, because of their transgression, salvation has come to the Gentiles, to make Israel envious.

In a very real sense, for even the dominant society church in America, we are undeserving of anything God has done for us. According to this passage, the rebellion of the Israelites, and their subsequent rejection of Christ as the Messiah meant that salvation was opened up for the rest of the world.

Salvation needs to be understood in this context: The Jews first, and also the Greeks (rest of the Gentile world).

If the North American church would realize that the gospel

did not originate in the United States and Canada, but has its roots in Jerusalem, it would revolutionize our understanding of world missions.

In fact, the gospel did begin in the community of Jerusalem, and just like Christ said, it went into all Judea, which was the province in which Jerusalem was located in, and from there to Samaria, which was a neighboring province made up of half-breed Jews, and then to the uttermost parts of the earth.

I have often told Anglo churches that you can't get much farther from Jerusalem than the United States of America! In the biblical sense, we are actually the end of the earth, the boon-docks, and the foreign field! I have also said to them, "have you ever thought that you should be the ones on the slides, rather than the ones watching the slides of the foreign field when missionary conference time rolls around!"

But the average North American Christian does not see missions from that perspective. He often will have the view that "we are the sending church," and everything that is happening in the world comes out of America. There might even be a bit of prideful boasting that the American church would have to admit being guilty of, when the church in America evaluates itself.

Paul said to the Romans, it would be better to feel grateful to the Lord that salvation has come to you, rather than feeling proud and boastful over what you have accomplished!

He goes on to develop an analogy of the worldwide Church of Christ to that of an olive tree, and oh, are there some important principles listed for us.

He says in verses 17-24,

If some of the branches have been broken off, and you, though a wild olive shoot, have been grafted in among the others, and now share in the nourishing sap from the olive root, do not boast over those branches. If you do, consider this: You do not support the root, but the root supports you. You will say then, "Branches were broken off so that I could be grafted in." Granted. But they were broken off because of unbelief, and you stand by faith. Do not be arrogant, but be afraid. For if God did not spare the natural branches, he will not spare you either. Consider therefore the kindness and sternness of God: sternness to those who fell, but kindness to you, provided that you continue in his kindness. Otherwise, you also will be cut off. And if they do not persist in unbelief, they will be grafted in, for God is able to graft them in again. After all, if you were cut out of a olive tree that is wild by nature, and contrary to nature were grafted into a cultivated olive tree, how much more readily will these, the natural branches, be grafted into their own olive tree!

The analogy in this passage is obvious, and so is its implications to all of us who are Gentile by birth.

We need to be reminded that when God sees the world, He basically sees two types of people, the believer and the unbeliever. As it relates to His dealings with the people groups of the world, he established a special covenant with one group, the Israelites, with whom He has shared a special relationship and will do so even through the end times of the ages. After saying all that, Scripture reminds us that God is no respecter of persons, and that He really sees a world where there is neither Jew nor Gentile, slave or free, but He sees us all on an equal basis. Many Christians just don't have that mind-set, nor do Native American people view biblical spirituality in this way either.

I believe that there is a message to both dominant society believers in Christ, and for Native Christians as well, found in this passage.

Paul makes it clear about the details of this olive tree. The olive tree simply represents the worldwide Body of Christ, made up of believers from many tribes, peoples and nations. Every nation that has believers in Christ is represented as a branch on this olive tree. As you look at this tree, you will see that near it are branches, that were the natural branches from this tree, broken off, lying dormant on the ground, separated from the life-giving sap that comes from the root. Those broken off branches represent the Israelites, who were broken off because of unbelief.

The root is Christ, Himself, and it is His life and power that flows up through the trunk of the tree and nourishes every branch that is there, whether it is the natural ones or the grafted ones.

All other cultures of the world are represented by the grafted branches that adorn this tree. Those of us who, though wild by nature, have been grafted in, should not boast in anything we do, because that would be contrary to why God has grafted us in the first place. This was His admonition to the Gentiles in Rome who were walking about somewhat prideful that they had taken the place of unbelieving Jews in this Roman congregation.

As you look at this tree, you see these grafted branches in all different stages of growth and development. You see a large, fruitful branch, which could represent the American church, and it looks strong and established—even though it too was grafted in, though wild by nature. Around the other side of the tree you will see perhaps smaller branches, representing other cultures that have been more recently grafted in, while further up the trunk you will see a small twig, that is still held onto the trunk by the twine that keeps it in place.

The lesson of not boasting to stronger, more established branches are contrasted with the lesson for the Native American Body of Christ. That lesson is this: We're there!

The blessing of this passage to me as a Native American is that we have been grafted into the worldwide Body of Christ, though wild by nature, along with every other branch that is there, including the church made up believers from the dominant society. Also, the reminder that we don't support the root, but the root supports us is a tremendous lesson for the Native American branch! We are tapped into the same source of enablement that any other branch, including the strong, powerful, influential American church is tapped into, the nourishing sap that comes from the root of the tree, Christ, Himself!

We need to be reminded in the Native church that the source for our support, power and enablement is not to come from any other branch, but it comes by our abiding in the nourishing sap that comes from the root. How does this effect the local American church as it views its involvement in world missions?

It should serve as a reminder of the need for humility, and

not boasting, because, though wild by nature, God has granted them the privilege of being grafted into the Body of Christ, and should see itself in just that light. That speaks to the motivation for ministry.

When that happens, a whole world of possibilities open up and missionary work worldwide would experience a tremendous revival and renewed empowerment from the root. Remember the admonition. No branch should consider itself as the support supply to the rest of the Body of Christ. Only the root can supply that.

I think it also calls on the church to realize that, unless we are Jewish by birth, we are all products of missions, including all Gentile branches!

When we approach missions from that perspective, our motivation will be to truly go to the regions beyond, and our own backyard, with a sense of gratitude to the Lord that He has allowed me to be grafted in. In humility and in a way that does not boast, we should serve the world with the gospel of Jesus Christ. That, in my opinion, is how we all should approach our service in the Kingdom of God.

1   Vine Deloria, Jr. *Custer Died for Your Sins* (University of Oklahoma Press) Third Printing 1989 Page 118.

2   Ibid, Pages 112,124

Now those who had been scattered by their persecution in connection with Stephen traveled as far as Phoenicia, Cyprus and Antioch, telling the message only to the Jews. Some of them, however, men of Cyprus and Cyrene, went to Antioch and began to speak to the Greeks also, telling the good news about the Lord Jesus. The Lord's hand was with them, and a great number of people believed and turned to the Lord.

News of this reached the ears of the church at Jerusalem, and they sent Barnabas to Antioch. When he arrived and saw the evidence of the grace of God, he was glad and encouraged them all to remain true to the Lord with all their hearts. He was a good man, full of the Holy Spirit, and faith, and a great number of people were brought to the Lord.

Then Barnabas went to Tarsus to look for Saul, and when he found him, he brought him to Antioch. So for a whole year Barnabas and Saul taught great numbers of people. The disciples were called Christians first at Antioch.

During this time some prophets came down from Jerusalem to Antioch. One of them, named Agabus, stood up and through the Spirit predicted that a severe famine would spread over the entire Roman world. (This happened during the reign of Claudius). The disciples, each according to his ability, decided to provide help for the brothers living in Judea. This they did, sending their gift to the elders by Barnabas and Saul.

In the Church in Antioch there were prophets and teachers: Barnabas, Simeon called Niger, Lucius of Cyrene, Manaen (who had been brought up with Herod the tetrarch) and Saul. While they were worshipping the Lord and fasting, the Holy Spirit said, "Set apart for me Barnabas and Saul for the work to which I have called them." So after they had fasted and prayed, they placed their hands on them and sent them off.

—Acts 11:19-30, 13:1-3

Chapter 5

The

Antioch Model

ONE OF THE MOST interesting accounts of the establishment of a local church recorded in all of Scripture is this account of the church in Antioch.

There are several things that immediately stand out in my mind as significant. First, we are reminded that the believers were called Christians first in Antioch.

What was so special about this church that would finally qualify them to be called "Christian?" Something happened with the Antioch believers that allowed them to bear that name, a name that has withstood the test of time, and is the name we still use today to designate followers of Jesus Christ.

I call myself a Christian. I belong to a church that is Christian. I attempt to live my life based on values that are Christian. Based upon these realities, I think it is important to me to study Antioch, because something happened there so as to qualify the believers to bear that name.

The interesting thing is that prior to Antioch, there were many believers in Christ, but they weren't called Christians. On the day of Pentecost alone, when the church was born, there were thousands that accepted Christ, and many thousands more up to

Antioch, but none of them were called Christians.

The church in Antioch is a tremendous model for us in Native ministry, because no other church planting endeavor recorded in Scripture has as many parallels with the challenge of Native ministry than Antioch.

The lessons for the Native church from Antioch are many. If we would develop our Native churches following the Antioch model, I believe we would experience stronger and more dynamic Native churches, and we would be able to break out of the outdated and ineffective mold that has been set for centuries, since the gospel first came to our land.

The way the ministry began in Antioch sets the stage for the rest of the development of this church.

The climate of the day among the early days of the church was such that many Jewish believers had not yet bought into the command of Christ to cross over into Gentile cultures and share the blessing of salvation. In fact, shortly before the ministry began in Antioch, Peter had his vision on the roof top of Simon the tanner's home, which instructed him to go beyond his cultural comfort zone and preach Christ to whoever would listen. In going from Simon the tanner's roof top to Cornelius, the Italian centurion's home, Peter not only crossed Jewish terrain, he crossed Jewish tradition, which forbade the Jews to even mingle with Gentiles.

In the context of that kind of racial climate, the church in Antioch was born.

I again want to remind us that though we share many similarities with the Israelites, we also must learn from their mistakes and not duplicate them as we seek to develop a strong biblical Native church. We must see that our responsibility includes being culturally sensitive to other cultures, and be involved in extending our ministries outside of our own cultural comfort zones, too.

Antioch was situated in the far north of Syria. It was there that, after Stephen was stoned for his faith, some of the Jewish believers scattered, with some making their way to this important and busy northern capital, which was where the Europeans and Asiatic people met, and Greek civilization touched the Syrian desert.

When the ministry originally began in Antioch, it was doomed to failure, for it says that when the first arriving "missionaries" came to Antioch, they preached Christ to none but the Jews only. They felt the message was for just those from their own culture and racial heritage.

Scripture does not give us a recording of the success that they had in this endeavor. Why? I fully believe that Scripture could not give an account of success because there was no success to report on!

Antioch almost ended up a failure before it even got started.

It is only after other Jews, who when they came to Antioch, crossed over from their culture to another, and preached to the Greeks also, did the chance for success begin.

Scripture does give us a recording of their success, as it says in Acts 11:21 "a great number of people believed and turned to the Lord."

The church in Antioch was doomed to failure, unless they became cross-cultural in their outreach. How does this apply to us today?

The Gentile population was considered by the Jews to be from the other side of the tracks. You know, those "minority types." But it took the Jews reaching beyond their cultural comfort zone to begin to experience success in their ministry in Antioch. And that principle is for us today.

Churches in America that are not about the business of reaching out to other cultures are not going to experience the kind of success and blessing that comes from the Lord until they see the need to be cross-cultural.

In reality, comparing it to today, the church in Antioch actually would be considered a minority or "ethnic" church in light of the culture of the people bringing the message!

As it applies to us as Native Americans, it would be the same as some group coming to one of our communities, but not speaking about Christ to Native Americans, but only to the Anglo population in that community.

This model, unfortunately is seen all across America. There are strong, established Anglo churches all across America, many of whom are sitting right in the middle of, or right next door to, Native American populations. The problem is that they are preaching the message to none but their people only! From the experience of Antioch, if that is the case, these churches really are not going to experience the blessing of the hand of the Lord on them, until they reach out to all people around them.

This dynamic is best illustrated by what happened to church after church in the cities of our land. As the demographics of neighborhoods changed, and more "minority" people moved in, churches packed up, and moved out of those neighborhoods to the comfort zone of suburbia. Antioch, and cross-cultural outreach, was the farthest thing from their mind!

This passage lays before us one of the most important statements for the church today. It says in Acts 11:21 that when they crossed the culture, "The hand of the Lord was with them."

There is a spiritual truth that is as real today as it was back then, and that principle is this, if we are cross-cultural, we can expect to have the hand of the Lord on us! I wonder today if the hand of the Lord is upon the church as mightily as it should be, especially as it relates to the flight of church after church from the cities to the suburbs.

But it also has implications for us as Native Americans and for our Native churches.

If we are to experience the hand of the Lord and his blessing on our ministry, we too must become cross-cultural!

As I said in an earlier chapter, much of the missionary work done among our people has been historically done out of motivation based on our plight or problems, and not our potential. That is why missionaries have never really taught Native Americans to become cross-cultural. Had this happened, we would have long ago moved from the receiving end of all of the giving, helps and involvement of the Anglo American church, to that of participators. We would be the ones to go, to give, to cross over, and in doing so, reach our full potential for Christ.

I truly and honestly believe that the church has done a great disservice to the Native Americans who have become Christians over the centuries by keeping them on the receiving end of ministry. Even to this day, much of the mindset and motivation of many ministries among Native people perpetuates and keeps us as the receivers.

The time has come for us, however, as Native American Christians, to take our responsibility seriously and become cross-cultural in our churches.

Let me ask you, if you are a Native Christian, do you feel responsible for reaching the world with the gospel? Or do you feel that it is the responsibility of the Anglo church alone, because they have the resources and personnel to do the job?

If that is your thinking, then you will not experience fully the blessing and hand of the Lord in your life and church. Remember, God's greatest work is done through the underdogs!

Once this church began to grow rapidly, news of this amazing work reached the ears of the national denominational leadership back in Jerusalem.

Just like our denominations of today, they sent the denominational representative from the national office, brother Barnabas, to go and see if they were doing everything according to the denominational policies and procedures! I'm sure the leadership thought this was not the case, especially because they were reaching out to, you know, those Gentiles!

I'm glad they sent Barnabas, because God was working in his heart regarding this major shift of thinking, that even those minority people should be included in the propagation of the gospel. The name "Barnabas" means 'son of encouragement.' He came with his heart and mind wide open.

When he got to Antioch and saw this ethnic church instead of a Jewish church, he was glad, and did much to encourage them on in their faith.

He decided to stay there, and begin the process of disciple-ship, which was so important to the grounding of these new believers in their faith. Realizing that he couldn't do it alone, he went to Tarsus to get Saul, who was sitting on the shelf over there for what might have been as much as ten years. Everyone was scared of Saul, and didn't trust this former persecutor of the Church to be sincere in his conversion. But not Barnabas. This positive leader of the church thought to himself, "This is just the kind of man I need to help establish the church in Antioch."

He brought Saul back to Antioch, and Scripture says that for a whole year, they taught the new, ethnic church, this church that almost never got started, in their faith.

Earlier, I mentioned that there were some missionaries work-ing among our people who did exemplary work, giving their lives in service to our people, and their legacies live on to this day. They, like Barnabas and Saul, ministered based on a motivation that saw the potential, and not the problems of the people they served.

In many ways, the church has had a history, in its work among Native Americans, to count success in terms of "converts," rather than in terms of "making disciples." It has proven easy, over the course of time, to get Native Americans to "accept Christ," or recite a creed, but it was not the strong point of many ministries to take a Native convert and go through the agonizing process of making that person a true follower of Christ. The impor-tance of discipleship was overlooked, or improperly taught, by all too many working among our people.

It amazed me when, back in the early 1980s I went with my local Native pastor on some home visits throughout my reserva-tion to find the large number of local Native people who at one time or another had accepted Christ, through the missionary work of early pioneers, but were in no way living for Christ to-day, and had not for years.

Some missionaries among our people, however, knew the principles of Saul and Barnabas. They were committed to the important ministry of discipleship, and mentoring. They taught their converts that not only did God want to use them but they were encouraged to step out and do things for Christ.

Because of this solid discipleship teaching, Native converts such as my grandparents, helped establish ministries like the "Chippewa Bible Broadcast," a radio program that was on the air, preaching and teaching in the Chippewa language, for more than twenty-six years.

Now I wish I had an 800 toll-free number to call and plant down my credit card and order Saul and Barnabas' teaching tapes. Man, I would even pay the big bucks to get the videos!

I wish we had their materials for use in our Native churches. Why? Because of the results of their discipleship teaching ministry. Some applied these principles found in Antioch as they have ministered on reservations across North America. When successful missionaries among Native Americans presented Christ to our people in a way that was powerful, effective, and culturally relevant, the end result has been Native Christians who were not only won to Christ, but became disciples of Christ, and their testimonies live on today in the lives of generations that have also walked with the Lord.

I know that I would not be serving the Lord today, had it not been for the effective discipleship ministry some of the early C&MA missionaries had among my grandparents. Their stand for Christ was solid, and now in our family we have four generations of Christians! That's the power of effective missionary work and faithfulness.

The passage continues that after this new, ethnic church plant was only one year old, some other denominational representatives, with the gift of prophecy, came to Antioch. They prophesied that there was going to be a great famine, all throughout the Roman world, and it was going to be bad. It would affect Palestine, Syria, and all over, including Antioch.

The response of the new ethnic believers in Antioch is a testimony to the teaching and discipling ministry of Saul and Barnabas. We read that after the disciples in the Antioch church heard about the famine which was going to affect even them:

*The disciples, each according to their ability, decided to provide help
for the brothers living in Judea. This they did, sending their gift to the
elders by Barnabas and Saul.*

Acts 11:29-30

Can you imagine that this Antioch church, which almost never
got started because they were preaching to only their own kind
and God wasn't blessing, became a strong established minority
church, that moved in one year's time from a new infant church
to one that when a need was presented, became the participators, reaching out to others! After only one year!

Saul and Barnabas' motivation for their discipleship ministry
was based on the potential of this rag tag bunch of people from
the other side of the tracks, and not on their plight or problems.
This motivation affected their discipleship ministry to such an
extent that they were able to move this new minority church
from the receiving end of missions, to the participation end of
missions in such a short time.

If this scenario was played out in North America, among
Native Americans, more likely than not the missionaries would
feel compelled to approach the big support churches to help out
the mission station on the reservation, because of these hard
times. That is plight motivated missions as it has been normally
done among our people.

We have had ministry among Native Americans for centuries, and we are still on the receiving end! What a tragedy! And it
all goes back to the motivation that is based on the plight and
not the potential of Native people. It goes back to the mentality
that I shared in an earlier chapter about the denominational representative who told his Native constituency, just worry about
Native Americans, and leave the rest of the world to us!

If we as the Native church are going to experience the hand
of the Lord, then we need to take it upon ourselves to become
cross-cultural. I think it's a shame that we have had to discover
this biblical truth on our own, centuries after the gospel came
here, but discover it we have, and now the responsibility lies on

our shoulder. What are we going to do about this biblical concept that up to this point has not been taught to us?

Let me share what I believe is a good first place to start, again, using the Antioch church as our model.

When Agabus told of the famine which was to come, the Antioch believers provided the principle for us to follow.

First, it says that every person, according to his ability, determined to do something.

Let's start there. I would challenge every Native believer, whether you have little, or whether you have much, to accept the biblical truth that God's hand will be on you and bless you when you reach out beyond your people, and bless someone of another culture or race.

In fact, a good place to start is where the Antioch believers started. Who were the recipients of Antioch's offerings? It says they sent their gifts to the brothers living in Judea. Now let me ask you, who were the "brothers living in Judea." What cultural group lived in Judea? Why it was none other than the Jews! And by the way, who were the people who, when they came to Antioch didn't even include the Gentiles in their initial sharing of the gospel? The Jews.

One of the most dynamic principles of spiritual maturity and growth is demonstrated by whom the Antioch church chose to bless. They chose to bless the very ones that did them wrong, by not even considering them worthy of the gospel when they first came to Antioch. This principle, if followed in our Native churches, and all churches for that matter, will break long standing barriers and walls of division between our people and those who have done us wrong. This principle applies to any individual or group that has been victimized by any other group. Be a blessing to those who have done you wrong! Do something tangible to those who have hurt you in the past, and in so doing, God's hand and blessing will be on you in ways that will repay you and bless you many times over.

Antioch chose to bless those brothers living in Judea. For us as Native Americans, why don't we determine, every Native

Christian, according to each of our abilities, to cross over the wide canyon of past atrocities, pain and mistreatment, and, in a tangible way, bless those who have done us wrong, and see what God will do!

I am convinced that when we become cross-cultural, and shoulder our part of the responsibility to be world Christians, God's blessing and hand will be on us as we have never experienced before in the Native American branch of the olive tree!

But you know, it's not just a message for the Native church and Native people. We all need to be reminded that God won't bless us if we hold hatred and animosity toward those of other cultures and colors, and the best way to get beyond those hurts and pains of the past, is to be a blessing to those who have done you wrong!

There is one other item that I want to draw from the Antioch church that is important for us today. That item is the response of cross-culturally sensitive churches to go into all the world.

As the church in Antioch grew and developed, Acts 13:1-2 reminds us that there was a plurality of leaders that developed there. It says, *In the church at Antioch there were prophets and teachers: Barnabas, Simeon called Niger, Lucius of Cyrene, Manaen (who had been brought up with Herod the tetrarch) and Saul.*

Not only is it exciting to see that this church, in a very short time was able to grow and develop so that a plurality of leadership developed. As important and exciting as the fact that there was a plurality of leadership was the realization that this leadership was a virtual rainbow of color and culture. It was a true reflection of God's complete Body of Christ, allowing leaders to come from a variety of cultural upbringing! No wonder they were called Christians first at Antioch!

First, it says that there was Barnabas, who was Jewish, and he represented the leadership from Jerusalem. Simeon, called Niger, was Black, while Lucius of Cyrene was probably a Greek. Manaen would have been an aristocrat, and quite possibly an Essene, since he had been brought up with Herod the tetrarch, and then there was Saul, a marginal (living straddling the fence of two cultures) Jew. What a tremendous picture of what God desires to see in leadership within His Body!

As they were involved in their leadership responsibilities of worship, fasting and prayer, the Holy Spirit called Barnabas and Saul to leave Antioch, and begin what was to become known in Scripture as their first missionary journey. To that end they were faithful, and after being commissioned by the church in Antioch, they went out and did just that.

Imagine, this minority church, this underdog church, this church that almost never got started in the first place, became the center of the missionary activity of the church as recorded in Acts. In fact, when they completed their first missionary journey, Scripture says that they returned, not to Jerusalem, but to Antioch, and assembled the believers there and had their first missionary convention, complete with slides, curios and filmstrips, I'm sure!

This illustrates again to me, the potential of the underdogs, when we make ourselves available to be used by God. He longs to use us, He longs to bless us, and He longs to give to the world His message through us in a very unique way. This is based upon our own journey through life as those who are not noble, not influential, not mighty, based on the standards of, and in comparison to, the powerful nations of the world.

Let me share as clearly as I can that the Native church, in order to experience the full blessing of God, must involve itself in the commission that Christ gave his church just prior to his ascension. That commission is to go into all the world, and preach the gospel to all nations. We are just as responsible for that mandate as any other branch of the olive tree.

From my observations, not only can we do it, but I believe that world evangelization would be accelerated, when Native American missionaries go to the world. This principle, to me, has been the key missing link to the growth and establishment of a strong Native church.

As already mentioned, in my ministry I have had the unique

opportunity to go to a number of countries around the world.

As I have visited other countries, I have been amazed by the reception I have received, as a Native American, from the Native people of those lands. Let me give you just one illustration to make my point.

I was invited several years ago by the president of our denomination in Australia to speak at their annual national General Council meeting. Along with our ministry at this national conference, our team (I had my wife and father with me as our musical trio) was asked to stay on for several weeks to conduct evangelistic campaigns among the Aborigines in the outback of Australia.

It was a wonderful trip for us, and how we enjoyed the fellowship and camaraderie of the aboriginal Christians there. They are so much like the Native Americans in so many ways. They have the same kind of humor we as Indians have, they love the country style singing, complete with guitars, drums and the like, and even have the same, not so steady 4/4 timing (what I call 4/4 and a half time) when they sing their songs. Though they have suffered much, they are in many ways survivors, and are making the best of their situation.

I remember when we were getting ready to go on this trip, the president of the Alliance in Australia, Roger Lang, faxed me some information. He mentioned that where they were sending us in the outback was very remote, desolate, and hot! He said, "You will be with us in February, which is the peak of our summer here. Where we are sending you in the outback, it has been known to get up to one hundred and fifty degrees!"

I faxed a letter back to Roger and said, "Thanks, Roger! I know that's hot, because that temperature is one of the settings on our oven!"

When we were in one of the most isolated parts of the outback, we visited in the office of an aboriginal company that raised oranges. Hanging on the wall was a piece of paper, with one of the most hilarious statements, which illustrates their humor. It is so much like Indian humor, I almost think we are from the same mold.

I asked if I could make a copy of that statement, and they said by all means. I brought this home with me and have shared it numerous times to many people. The statement read,

Dear White Fella;
Couple of things you ought to know -
> *Firstly,*
> *When I am born, I'm black,*
> *When I grow up, I'm black,*
> *When I go out ina sun, I'm black,*
> *When I'm cold, I'm black*
> *When I get scared, gee I'm black,*
> *When I die, I'm still black.*
> *But You White Fella,*
> *When you born, you pink,*
> *When you grow up, you white,*
> *When you get sick, you green*
> *When you go out ina sun, you red*
> *When you cold, you blue*
> *When you scared, you yellow,*
> *When you die, you purple!*
> *And you have the cheek to call me coloured!*

During the national conference, where both Australian and aboriginal churches were represented, I shared a message that incorporated the history of the Native Americans and all that we have suffered over the past centuries with the loss of our lands, culture, languages and identity, and spoke about my grandparents experiences in the government boarding schools.

After that message, the Aborigines rushed to the front and embraced me, saying to me, "Brother Smith, you were telling our story!" In many ways the history of the Australian Aborigines mirrors that of the Native American experience. That one message gave me a level of acceptance with them that was incredible.

In fact, an American missionary was observing this exchange

after the service and he pulled me aside. He told me, "You know, I have been here for years, and still have not been accepted by the Aborigines to the degree you now enjoy! You were able to accomplish, in one message, more than I have been able to accomplish in years being here."

It caused me to begin thinking of how missionary work worldwide would be accelerated if Native Americans were actively involved.

Another denominational leader, and a good friend of mine was a missionary in Brasilia, Brazil. He told me once about how hard it was for American missionaries to break through the barriers of acceptance in that country. The native people there, he said, look at us as "Imperialist Americans." But if a Native American was to come to Brasilia, he commented, he would not come with the same cultural baggage, but would be immediately accepted by the Brazilian native people.

In Acts 13:47 we read,

I have made you a light to the Gentiles, that you may bring salvation to the ends of the earth.

The real motivation for the Body of Christ to evangelize Native Americans lies in this verse, especially when we look beyond the obvious truth to the deeper truth that lies somewhat hidden from just the casual view.

The obvious truth revealed in this verse is that when we go to the Gentiles, we are bringing salvation to the ends of the earth.

The deeper truth, I believe is this. When we go to the Gentiles (i.e. Native Americans), we reach them so that they too will become involved and aid in the process of taking the gospel to the ends of the earth. This must be the motivating factor in why we do missionary work among any tribe worldwide, so that they will move from beyond the recipient of missions to that of the participator. That holds true for the missionary working among the professionals of some European country to those working among the Stone Age tribes of Irian Jaya. Oh, and just a reminder, the cultures that we look at as the most backward, and unlearned are the ones that God wants to use to do some amazing things worldwide through!

Here are just a few of the advantages that I believe we as Native Americans bring to the table of world evangelization.

First, we do bring an "underdog" mentality to missions. As already has been stated, God uses underdogs through which to do some amazing work.

Secondly, we often will have a natural affinity with the Native inhabitants in the countries we would go to. This would provide the potential of accelerated acceptance, and open up the gospel more quickly to resistant and hardened people.

Thirdly, Native Americans have an understanding of the spirit world that is very similar to that of many animistic people groups world wide. Our understanding of the powers and even identity of spiritual forces and how they work would help the Church provide the full message of the gospel, including not only salvation, but deliverance from the powers of darkness. This understanding of the spirit world is somewhat foreign to the typical American missionary, until he is confronted with these forces on the field.

Fourth, I believe we have the ability to do hard ministry with limited resources. That is the norm for us in most Indian work, because denominations have not always adequately funded Native American ministries, nor had it as a major priority. Our workers have often conducted their ministries with less pay and fewer resources for ministry than others doing comparable work in other parts of the same denomination. We know how to do much with very little. To us, that's the norm.

The principles of the Antioch Church are ones that we need to apply today, not only in Native American work, but in the worldwide work of the Body of Christ.

We must be cross-cultural to experience the hand of the Lord on our ministry, we must move quickly from the receiving end of ministry to the participating end, and we must tangibly reach out and be a blessing to even those who have done us wrong in the past, and make His last command our first concern.

I live for the day when we will be seeing missionaries sent out from our Indian churches to be a blessing and reach the world with the gospel of Jesus Christ. When that happens, world evangelization will be enhanced, expanded, and enlarged.

Chapter 6

Christianity

and

Indian Culture

ANOTHER MAJOR AREA of consideration, if we are going to dispel the fallacy that the gospel is the "Whiteman's Gospel," is to examine the notion that to be a Christian, you have to forsake all of your Native identity.

As we have already discussed, the history of Christianity among Native Americans has not been all that positive, and the message of Christ often misrepresented to our people. The message of Christ has not been given serious consideration by most Native people, because we have suffered so much by the methods that were used in the propagation of the gospel.

That redemption for Native people was viewed primarily as horizontal, and Christianity was then viewed as becoming Americanized, has been one of the key factors keeping many of our people from Christ. We had to leave all of our culture and identity behind, in order to be proper Christian people. The major mistake of this mentality is that the gospel of Jesus Christ never had the opportunity of meeting the Native person right where he was, with all his culture, language and identity. It never was given that chance.

Which brings us to the dilemma of the day. We have lost so

much of our culture, identity and languages, that our present Indian culture is definitely not what it traditionally was centuries ago. As we seek to contextualize the gospel to present day Indian culture, you run into a great diversity of differing levels of culture, all the way from very traditional to highly assimilated Native people. Pure Ojibwa culture is hard to find anymore, as is the case with many other tribes in North America.

How do we apply biblical principles now to a people that have lost so much of their identity and culture, and are continually being pressured to conform to the ways outside of our culture, as diluted as it often is?

Just what is the definition of culture? What makes up a person's identity? Well, here's what the dictionary has to say.

The civilization of a given people or nation at a given time or over all time; its customs, its arts, its conveniences.

Customs: any usual action or practice; habit; the accepted way of acting in a community or other group; tradition; or a long established habit that has almost the force of law. An action or way of doing things that has become established by a person or a group as the result of being repeated over a period of time.

Art: any form of human activity that is the product of and appeals primarily to the imagination ....drawing, painting, and sculpture, architecture, poetry, music and dancing.

Conveniences: all the effects, ways, and tools of a people used to accomplish work and activity in an expedient fashion.

Two things strike me from the above definition of culture. It is defined both, "at a given time" and "over all time." The culture of Indian people in North America must be understood in these two categories, if we are to minister effectively in this day and age.

We have a historical culture, which is rooted deeply in the traditions and ways of our ancestors. But we also have a contemporary culture, which is definitely not the same as the days of old, as many of the values, ways, and traditions have been lost.

Let's look at the issue of culture "over all time," to give us a historical overview which will provide the foundation on which to examine the present day Indian culture.

The Civilization of a People or Nation over All Time

First of all, it's important to realize that to deal with an overview of Native culture historically is virtually impossible to do, because of the complexity and diversity of Indian culture. There were literally hundreds of tribes, with some being completely wiped out and no lasting record of their culture or traditions. There was also a great diversity of ancestral languages, and traditions, so to list them all would take volumes.

There also is, in a very real sense, little left in many tribes to pass on.

There are, however some blanket assertions that can be made about the Indian culture viewed over all time.

First, for all Native American tribes, there was a deep spiritual basis to their whole life. This is a different concept than that of the dominant society. The dominant society tends to compartmentalize all the different aspects of their life. The spiritual is in one compartment, separate from the social, as are the educational from the vocational, and so on.

To a traditional Native American, everything about his or her life and existence is spiritual. There was a common misconception for most early settlers, thinking that the Indians were without spiritual sensitivity or involvement. The truth of the matter is that historically, Native people are an extremely spiritually sensitive people.

Another characteristic of the traditional Indian was his reverence for the land. Indians refer to the earth as their "mother," and honor land with the same honor a mother is due. That is why the dominant society's concept of buying and selling land was foreign to the Native person. How do you cut up and sell your mother? It goes without saying that the Native American's traditional and early view was to share the land with the new arriving immigrants, and that mentality paved the way for land seeking expansionists to take advantage of our ancestors.

We were also self sufficient people, much in contrast to the many Native people of today who have been reduced to living in the welfare system as a way of life. Our skill and ability to provide for our families was unquestionable, and some of the early European settlers have the Native people to thank for helping them survive in their early days here.

We also can look back and see that historically, Native American culture included an organized society, much to the misunderstanding of many new immigrants. In fact, the United States Constitution is patterned after the great Iroquois Confederacy's system of government.

One of the main differences in the Indian and non-Indian communities is what we value, and hold on to as important. A part of Indian culture that has been and still is important to us was the role of the elders of our communities, and their responsibility of passing down from one generation to the next our oral tradition.

The Native's view of influence was based then, and still is today, on wisdom. It is what we placed high value and importance in. On the other hand, the European's view of influence and power was, and continues to be, based on knowledge. That's why in Indian culture we place great value and honor on our elders, for they are the ones with great wisdom that comes from the experiences of life, and it is from them we learn and perpetuate our heritage.

On the other hand, that's why the Anglo community, even to this day, places such a high value on formal education, and the pursuit of degrees that qualify you for jobs, advancement and honor. It is through such educated individuals that the traditions, values and culture of the Anglo community will be perpetuated.

Neither view is right nor wrong, or necessarily more important than the other, and each one has its benefits. You can have all kinds of knowledge about many things, but not possess the wisdom of what to do with such knowledge! That's why both are needed to fill out our lives. It reminds me of the old saying, "His understanding of life was a mile wide, but only an inch deep!" Knowledge expands your breadth of understanding. Wisdom expands your depth of understanding.

As far as gospel ministry is concerned, the strong point of the one culture (Indians = Wisdom, Anglo = Knowledge), ended up being the weak point of the other.

Where does wisdom come from?

In the Old Testament, a man named Job asks and answers that question. In Job 28:12, he asks, "But where can wisdom be found? Where does understanding dwell?" He answers that question in chapter 12:12. He says, "Is not wisdom found among the aged? Does not long life bring understanding?"

Though Native Americans value and possess wisdom, they lacked the knowledge of true Christianity to make the wise choice of following Christ. Just like I mentioned in Chapter One, Native people have great zeal for their concept of God, but that zeal is not based on Scriptural knowledge of God's plan of redemption. I really believe that if our ancestors were presented with the pure, unadulterated gospel message, and not shrouded in the culture of the arriving immigrants, our people would have been wise enough to respond.

In fact, there are enough stories in different tribal legends of Native people seeing visions, prior to the arrival of the Europeans, of people described as white men in "black coats," coming to bring the message of truth, to validate the fact that our people were to a degree prepared to receive the message of the gospel, once it arrived here.

On the other hand, though the Europeans possessed and regarded knowledge as supreme, what they lacked, and sometimes still do, was wisdom in the presentation of the gospel to Native Americans. If the gospel is to be embraced by any culture, the culture of the people being reached needs to be respected, for it is much easier for God to convict than it is for man to try and do the work of the Holy Spirit. The power of the gospel is complete in and of itself to penetrate a culture, and redeem that which is redeemable, and convict and deal with that which is animistic and abominable in nature.

What a shame it was that historically all of the culture and ways of our people were considered so heathen and pagan by the new arriving immigrants. We must admit that there are parts of all cultures that under careful biblical scrutiny, can only be described as animistic and abominable to God, but I do not feel that all of Indian culture can be classified as such.

The Civilization Of A People At A Given Time

We also need to look at today's Native person, because the Native of today is in many ways different from his ancestors. We have been strongly influenced by outside forces, causing our societies to move from what we once were, to what we now are. Those who minister to the Indian person of today have to understand the culture and mind set of the contemporary Indian person if he is to be reached effectively with the gospel.

What is contemporary Indian culture? What does it mean today to be an Indian? How is the gospel to effectively be promoted in light of the mistakes of the past, and the challenge of the present?

What we do find today is a very complex, and diverse make up of Indian life, ways, and mannerisms in our contemporary society. Not only do we have hundreds of tribes still alive today, each with their own distinct cultures, we have many subcultures within each of those tribes, clans, and even family units.

What does it mean, today, to be an Indian? For some, that term has been rejected in favor of Native, Aboriginal, or First Nations. While many others still feel comfortable with the name Indian, when identifying themselves.

In Canada, they, by and large, have rejected the term Indian, and use the terms, "Aboriginal," and also "First Nations." That changes everything! They can no longer call their cars, "Indian Cars." I guess they will have to call them "Aboriginal Automobiles," or "First Nation Fords!"

What then are the general identifying marks of our present Native culture and societies?

I think that first of all, one of the marks of our present Indian society is a stronger tribal identity.

Since the early 1970s, there was a shift of thinking that began where finally, it was O.K. to be an Indian. The damaging effects of the government boarding school era seemed far off in the distant past, and the negative feelings that abounded for almost one hundred years began to be replaced by a renewed pride in being Indian.

Along with Indian people themselves sensing a renewed pride in being Indian, there were a growing number of whites who wanted all Indians to know that in their family ancestry, they too have Indian blood! Someone in their past was "full-blooded Indian!" Why is it that people use the term "full blooded" when only referring to Indians?! I have never heard a white man say "I'm a full-blooded white man!"

When I see someone coming, who I know is going to tell me of their Indian ancestry, I try to beat them to the punch, because I know that they are going to tell me that their great-grandmother was a Cherokee princess. I try to tell them before they can get it out, "My great-grandmother was the Princess of Wales!"

I think Vine Deloria, Jr., articulated best the unique phenomena of many Americans desiring to have some tie with the Native people of this land. He says,

During my three years as Executive Director of the National Congress of American Indians it was a rare day when some white didn't visit my office and proudly proclaim that he or she was of Indian descent.

Cherokee was the most popular tribe of their choice and many people placed the Cherokees anywhere from Maine to Washington State. Mohawk, Sioux, and Chippewa were next in popularity. Occasionally I would be told about some mythical tribe from lower Pennsylvania, Virginia, or Massachusetts which had spawned the white standing before me.

At times I became quite defensive about being a Sioux when these white people had a pedigree that was so much more respectable than mine. But eventually I came to understand their need to identify as partially Indian and did not resent them. I would confirm their wildest stories about their Indian ancestry and would add a few tales

*of my own hoping that they would be able to accept themselves someday
and leave us alone.*

*Whites claiming Indian blood generally tend to reinforce mythical
beliefs about Indians. All but one person I met who claimed Indian
blood claimed it on their grandmother's side. I once did a projection
backward and discovered that evidently most tribes were entirely female for the first three hundred years of white occupation. No one, it
seemed, wanted to claim a male Indian as a forebear.*

*It doesn't take much insight into racial attitudes to understand
the real meaning of the Indian-grandmother complex that plagues
certain whites. A male ancestor has too much of the aura of the
savage warrior, the unknown primitive, the instinctive animal, to
make him a respectable member of the family tree. But a young
Indian princess? Ah, there was royalty for the taking. Somehow the
white was linked with a noble house of gentility and culture if his
grandmother was an Indian princess who ran away with an intrepid
pioneer. And royalty has always been an unconscious but all-consuming goal of the European immigrant."*

Another mark of our present Indian society is a return to the
traditions and religions of our past.

Along with the growing movement from the 1970s to go back
and regain our identity as Indian people have been the renewed
push to go back to the traditions and rituals of the past. In some
areas, there is an ever expanding inclusion of not only traditional religions of a particular tribe, but a growing acceptance
of pan-Indian movements such as the Native American Church,
or the Peyote Movement, which had its origins in the Southwest,
but is now being embraced nationwide.

I had an interesting conversation one time, just before I left
my home reservation when we moved to Arizona to do church
planting.

I was speaking with one of our local Indian elders, a spiritual
leader among our people, and one who was well respected by
those in our tribe.

He shared with me his observations about the many younger
Indians, including my generation, that has been pushing and

moving back to embrace the traditional Indian way of life.

His comment to me was a real eye opener.

He said, "Craig, I am upset at the younger Indians I see who think they are going back to the old ways, simply because they are now dancing in the powwows and participating in the sweats, and burning the sweet grass. These people who are doing this don't realize it, but they are being misled about our traditional ways of life."

"To us older Indians," he said, "traditions of our people are much more than rituals. They first and foremost have everything to do with values."

"These people who are going back to the rituals such as the powwows and sweats, dishonor our ancestors because after they take their regalia off, or after they put their clothes on after a sweat, they go out and blow their minds on drugs and booze, sleep around with anyone that will have them, neglect the children that they have brought into the world, and have families that live in fear and abuse."

How true was the wisdom of this elder, who himself wasn't a Christian. So many of our people, "in search of their identity," have attempted to find themselves by going back to the traditions of our ancestors. But what this man said is so true. Tradition is much more than rituals. It is first and foremost values. What values we hold to in our life will dictate how we treat ourselves, and how we treat others.

That is why I find it not a problem for me to be a Christian, and still be an Indian. Christian values and traditional Indian values are very similar. But it must be understood that even if these two value systems clashed, I still would have to choose biblical values, if I was to live a life pleasing to my Creator. It just so happens that between the traditional value system and biblical value system lies many similarities.

If you look at the biblical admonitions on how to live, and follow them, you will be honest, you will be a hard worker, you will provide for your family, you will love your wife and be committed to her, you will love your children and provide for them, you will not abuse your body or others bodies, and on and on the comparable principles go.

As diverse as our Indian cultures are, and as strong an emphasis there now is to retain those traditions, we do need to see that within the same tribe, clans, and even nuclear Indian families, is truly a multiplicity of cultures.

My family is a good example. Within our family of five boys and a mom and dad is a diversity of culture from one brother to the next. I have one brother who culturally leans very strongly to the Anglo side, while others lean strongly to the Indian side. It's hard to figure out how five boys, raised under the same roof, can have such diverse outlooks and cultural comfort zones, but we do!

There also can be a stark difference between Urbanized versus Reservation Indians, who are from the same tribe.

What has basically transpired over the years in all of Indian America has been a systematic move along what I call an assimilation scale. Remember our definition previously of "Assimilation?"

To make like the people of a nation or other group in customs, viewpoint, character, or other attribute. The process by which immigrants or other newcomers become like the people they are around, adopting the attitudes and cultural patterns of the society into which they have come.

Look with me at this assimilation scale for a moment.

ASSIMILATION SCALE

●————————————————●————————————————●
TRADITIONAL   MARGINAL   ASSIMILATED

Each of us as Indians fit somewhere on the cultural assimilation scale. Where do you fit? To help us identify where we are on the scale, I have listed below some of the characteristics that would define a Traditional Indian, a Marginal Indian, and an

Assimilated Indian. First, let's try to identify the characteristics of a traditional Indian of today.

Traditional Indians

I really don't feel that we have very many truly traditional Indian people left. The extreme end of this scale would mean a Native person who lives in the same world as that of his ancestors, with little or no contact or influence from the outside world. He would speak his Native tongue exclusively, and be involved in the traditions, including values and rituals of his ancestors. These kinds of Indians are hard to find today, but there are a few around.

The further east you go in America, the more exposure the Native tribes have had to the outside world. The further south and west you go in America, especially in really remote areas of Navajo and other Southwestern nations, the more truly traditional people you will find.

There are some people among my wife's tribe, the Navajo, who live isolated from the rest of the world, speak the language exclusively (many of the older ones don't know but maybe a few words of English), live in their traditional hogans, and herd sheep as their livelihood, in much the same way as their ancestors. About the only difference now is they have traded their donkeys in for four wheel drive pickups.

Probably the easiest way to identify a traditional Indian is that he will always point with his lips! For those not familiar with Indian humor, don't worry about it, just read on.

Marginal Indians

Now marginal Indians are easier to spot and are much more numerous than the traditional Indian.

A marginal Indian basically lives straddling the fence of the Indian world and the white man's world. He may or may not speak his own tribal language, but does know English, and is able to communicate in the two worlds.

This person also can easily gravitate between the Indian world and the white man's world, and have a basic understanding and appreciation for the good in both worlds. I know some highly educated Native people that are really "Indianish" in their ways, and that would be a marginal person.

This person may be raised on the reservation, or may have been raised in the city, but is able to survive in either place. This person may be involved in traditional religion and rituals, or he may be a Christian, or, may be involved in syncretism, which is a blending of Christianity and traditional Indian religion.

Probably the best way to identify a marginal Indian is that he will probably, most of the time, point with his lips when he's around other Indians, but become more formal around the white man and point with his fingers! Again, if you don't understand, don't try, just read on.

Assimilated Indians

Then there is the Assimilated Indian person, and you can find a good number of Indian people that fall under this category today, too.

An assimilated Indian person is one who, no matter what degree of Indian blood he may have, is completely "Anglo" in his thinking, worldview and culture. This person would speak English fluently, and would not even know his tribal language. The assimilated Indian is one who was probably either adopted by a non-Indian family, and raised in the dominant society's culture, or if not formally adopted, was probably raised by someone outside the Indian community.

This person would be either a Christian, even nominally, as many Americans claim to be, or, he may be involved in some other form of faith, be agnostic or even atheistic. He does not relate in any way, nor sees little value in, the traditional values, religion and ways of his ancestors. This person may even deny his Indian ancestry and heritage, and have no desire to learn about his people.

The easiest way to identify an assimilated Indian in a crowd is to watch and see him point, because he will exclusively point with his fingers, not even knowing that this is why God created lips! That's O.K. if you don't understand this lip business, please, just read on.

A good exercise for each Native person reading this book would be to take the three types of Indian people listed above, using the definitions of each, and decide where you personally are on the cultural assimilation scale.

You should be able to write your own definition of yourself, based upon the descriptions listed above, and then fairly accurately mark the spot where you feel you fit.

You might be somewhere between a traditional and marginal person. Or, you may lean more to the assimilated side.

As we can see, there is great diversity in the culture of the modern day Native person. We need to ask ourselves then, based upon this diversity, how do we effectively reach a traditionalist, a marginal and an assimilated Indian person today.

I am thoroughly convinced that there has to be sensitivity, on the part of those ministering among our people, to the cultural identity and placement of each Native person, and the gospel has to meet that person at exactly the point he is at on that scale of assimilation.

An assimilated Indian person will be able to be reached in much the same manner as any other person from the dominant society in America. A marginal person will have issues that deal with the two worlds he is living in. If he is to trust Christ, that unique dual culture that he lives in will need to be evaluated in light of God's principles. In the same way, a traditionalist that comes to Christ will need to evaluate all of his culture, including his customs, arts and conveniences, in light of God's Word, and God's standards.

Which raises an issue that many Indian people bring up.

Some would say that in our traditional Indian religion we do worship the Creator, and only use items of creation as a vehicle by which to worship the Creator. The sun in the sun dance, the eagle, the peyote, etc., all are vehicles, and not ends in themselves.

The Bible has something very important to say in response to this statement.

For there is one God, and one mediator between God and men, the man Christ Jesus. 1 Timothy 2:5

What has happened, however, in the bringing of Christianity to our shores is that the white man brought a culturally adapted form of Christianity that had fit with the traditions and cultural morays of the old European countries. But just as the European people, over time had to evaluate their culture, including its customs, arts and conveniences, in light of God's Word, our Native cultures must be given the same opportunity.

The Old Testament Foundation

Christian ministry among Native Americans has often started and stayed in the New Testament. A history of the Israelites and their tribal and traditional ways was never really introduced to our people. Ministry to Native people would be enhanced if we could build on the strong parallels between our Native cultures and values and that of God's chosen people, the Israelites. If denominations, mission organizations and missionaries across Indian country would make it a point to teach and develop these analogies between Indians and the Israelites, I believe our people would have a greater willingness to give Christianity a hearing.

Up until now, about all that we have been presented with was that if we were going to accept Christ, we would have to forsake all our identity, and become not only Christian, but become like the people who brought the gospel here, not the people with whom the gospel message originated. We've got to develop the proper connection between Native people and Israel, rather than Native people and the Anglo-Saxon European immigrant to this land.

As noted earlier in Chapter One, among my tribe, there are strong analogies with the Hebrews of the Old Testament. Our tribe historically, in the legends and stories passed down in the traditional *Me-da-we-win* rites, had certain rules to guide our people which William Warren noted, "bears a strong likeness to the Ten Commandments given by God to Moses on Mt. Sinai."

We have our traditional stories that are so similar to the Old Testament experiences of the Hebrews, that this is the natural place to start, and begin developing further biblical truth that leads up to Christ and Calvary. We must start though, in the Old

Testament, for it is there that Native Americans will be able to see so much of themselves, in the lives of the Israelites, that we will be drawn to Christ and Calvary in a more relational way, and will move us away from the concept that the gospel is the Whiteman's Gospel.

Another reason we have this misconception about Christianity that says, "If you are going to be a Christian, you can no longer be an Indian," is because one important attitude was lacking in the presentation of the gospel to the Indian people of North America. That was Paul's attitude described in First Corinthians 9:19-23.

> *Though I am free and belong to no man, I make myself a slave to everyone, to win as many as possible. To the Jews, I became like a Jew, to win the Jews. To those under the law, I became like one under the law (though I am not free from God's law but am under Christ's law), so as to win those under the law. To the weak, I became weak, to win the weak. I have become all things to all men so that by all possible means I might save some. I do all this for the sake of the gospel, that I may share in its blessings.*

This is a tremendous example of assimilation for the sake of the gospel, but what happened here historically was exactly the opposite. The people target to be reached had to be forced to become like the ones who were trying to win them to Christianity. This is not the Biblical pattern for reaching people with the gospel!

Principles of the Kingdom of God

In order for us to right the wrongs of the past, and understand Christianity in the biblical sense, we need to revisit the principles of the Kingdom of God!

Scripture tells us that there are not only earthly cultures, societies and nations, but there is an ultimately higher Kingdom, whose influence and power will visit each culture that responds to Christ. That higher Kingdom is the Kingdom of God.

This higher Kingdom is the one in which all human cultures must conform to, if they are to experience the blessing and visitation of the Creator. Every human culture, Indian, White, Black,

or Yellow when it comes to Christ, must submit themselves to
this higher Kingdom. Remember, though, true Christianity is
not conforming one's culture to another human culture, because
we are all under the curse of sin, and sin affects all cultures. The
only Kingdom that is pure, holy and righteous is the Kingdom
of God, and it's guidelines for living are given to us through
Holy Scriptures.

I must reiterate this point to make sure it is understood. The
mistake the church made among Indian people in its efforts to
evangelize was when they tried to move us from our culture
horizontally to their society's sin-stained culture. Those damaging efforts replaced vertical redemption, where the Indian's ways
were to be brought under the authority of the principles of God's
Word and the higher Kingdom of God and its standards. The
statement must be made that in all cultures there is much that is
good, which can be sanctified and used in the new, higher Kingdom of God. Conversely, there are things, and perhaps many
things, in all cultures that are contrary to the teachings of the
Kingdom of God.Where and when these contrary cultural issues arise, they must be set aside for the sake of the higher Kingdom. The bottom line is the Bible must become our guide book,
and its words the final authority in this matter.

We must be careful, however, not to make as equally damaging a mistake, in a reactionary way to the mistakes of the past.
In our efforts to make Christ more palatable to Native people,
we are tempted to move in the opposite direction by embracing
the lost, or previously thrown out elements, of our old Native
sin-stained cultures. In doing so, we run the risk of pursuing a
rebirth of old animism, masquerading as a more cultural expression and form of Christian worship and faith. In our desire to
have Christ "look more Indian," enthusiasm could blind us to
spiritual sensitivity. The line must be drawn on what is permissible and what is clearly defined in Scripture as against the principles of the Kingdom of God.

One truth must be maintained, and that is this. Our pursuit
must be of Christ, and not culture. If culture is more consum-

ing in our lives than Christ, we are not living a balanced Christian life.

The main question that I see in this process is, who is to decide which Native American cultural issues are permissible in the Kingdom of God and which are not?

The ultimate answer to that question is the Spirit of God. First Corinthians 2:6-16 tells us,

> *We do, however speak a message of wisdom among the mature, but not the wisdom of this age or of the rulers of this age, who are coming to nothing. No, we speak of God's secret wisdom, a wisdom that has been hidden and that God destined for our glory before time began. None of the rulers of this age understood it, for if they had, they would not have crucified the Lord of glory. However, as it is written, 'No eye has seen, nor ear heard, no mind has conceived what God has prepared for those who love him', but God has revealed it to us by his Spirit. The Spirit searches all things, even the deep things of God. For who among men knows the thoughts of a man, except the man's spirit within him? In the same way no one knows the thoughts of God except the Spirit of God. We have not received the spirit of the world, but the Spirit who is from God, that we may understand what God has freely given us. This is what we speak, not in words taught us by human wisdom but in words taught us by the Spirit, expressing spiritual truths in spiritual words. The man without the Spirit does not accept the things that come from God for they are foolishness to him, and he cannot understand them, because they are spiritually discerned. The spiritual man makes judgments about all things, but he himself is not subject to any man's judgment: "For who has known the mind of the Lord that he may instruct him?" But we have the mind of Christ.*

God is ultimately able, by His Holy Spirit, to deal with us individually regarding our cultures and practices, whether we are traditional, marginal or assimilated. The church must understand this concept and be willing to give allowance for the level an individual is at on the cultural assimilation scale.

In the past, those who stood outside of the culture and ways of the Indian people were the ones who decided all that was

Indian was sinful, and needed to be abandoned. Language, all customs and traditions and values needed to be changed to the "white way" in order to civilize and Christianize Indians. That mentality needs to change.

If we are to be successful in ministry to Indians of today, we need to see that the primary responsibility of the Church is to preach biblical truth, which transcends all culture, and is timeless, and allow the Spirit of God to either convict or convince individuals, wherever they are on the assimilation scale, that their individual practices, views, or activities are right or wrong in the sight of a holy and just God.

We need to see the great diversity in the culture of Indian people of today. Not one single form or fashion of ministry is going to appeal to all spectrums of the assimilation scale. An assimilated Indian would probably feel very comfortable in an Anglo style worship service, singing the old hymns of the church. We cannot assume, however, that a traditionalist or even a marginal Indian would share the same comfort zone. How should a traditionalist sing and praise his God, should he become a Christian? In the same way an assimilated Indian Christian does? Probably not. What is permissible? What is not?

I believe the best person to decide how a traditional person conforms his life to biblical principles is the traditionalist, himself, under the guidance of the Holy Spirit! As the gospel penetrates into a traditionalist's life, we as the church need to allow the Spirit of God to work in his life in such a way that he will evaluate his cultural ways in light of Scripture. This process, however, must not be brought on him by someone not familiar with his particular situation. When we do, we are saying that the Spirit of God is not capable of transforming a life, and needs our help. Are we as the Church willing to let this process happen? Without it, we will never be relevant to the people we are trying to reach.

A good example of this is a friend of mine, who is a converted Navajo medicine man, named Pete Greyeyes. Pete came to Christ in 1974, after he was under great spiritual attack from other medicine men. His cattle and sheep were dying, his horses were dying, and his family was becoming increasingly ill with sickness that could not be identified. The medicine men working against Pete were even sending messages through owls that were sent to his hogan. These owls sat in the cedar trees around his hogan at night and spoke to him in the Navajo language.

"We are going to kill you, you, you," they would say to him in Navajo. He tried to shoot at them with his rifle, but they continued to torment him.

Finally realizing he was powerless against these attacks, he came to the Navajo Mountain Alliance Church where my father-in-law, Rev. Herman Williams was preaching. He came at the end of a Sunday evening service. At the end of that service he came and committed his life to Christ.

Herman spent all night long counseling him in his new life in Christ. Finally, Pete told Herman about the owls, and asked, "What should I do?" I don't think any seminary in America would equip a pastor in how to deal with that question!

But again, Indians value wisdom, and Herman was a man full of the wisdom of God.

He simply told Pete, "If the owls can speak to you in Navajo, then they can listen to you in Navajo. Go back, and give them your testimony, and then tell them to get lost in Jesus' name!"

Pete did exactly that, and when he went home to his hogan, which was some thirty miles away over rough terrain, the owls were waiting for him.

Pete got out and preached his first sermon! I don't think the offering was very good, but the message was powerful.

He talked to the owls, and told them, "You owls have been tormenting me and my family. Last night I went to Navajo Mountain, and I accepted Jesus Christ as my Savior! All that I have, I have given to Him, including all this land, my hogan, my family, my livestock, everything. You are trespassing on God's property, so in the name of Jesus Christ, I command you to go!"

One by one those owls left, and to this day they have never returned. His family was supernaturally and dynamically healed, and the spiritual forces arrayed against him were defeated, all in the name of Jesus Christ.

How then should a Pete Greyeyes begin his walk in Christ? We cannot change the fact that Pete was raised traditionally, just like we can't change how each of us were raised culturally. But we do know that God can and did meet Pete, not only in the midst of his great need, but in the midst of his own personal culture, upbringing and way of life.

Pete's life, culturally, was completely traditional. It still is, even though he has been a Christian since 1974. Within the blanket of his culture, were parts that can only be described as animistic. When he became a Christian, those parts of his life needed to be put aside for the sake of Christ, and he was more than willing to do so. The positive result of putting away the animistic aspects of his culture was that he was delivered from the power and the fear of the spirit world that had consumed him throughout his life. But Pete still is a traditional Navajo. That hasn't changed. The parts of his culture that were not animistic in nature were presented to God, so that he could redeem that which was redeemable.

One of the things Pete explained about his former way of life was the belief of the medicine men that the spirit world was just beyond the reach of their outstretched hands. How surprised he was as he began reading Scripture as he read about "lifting holy hands without wrath to the Lord," and other verses that paralleled his traditional ways. Biblical concepts were introduced and embraced, through his traditional Navajo culture and mindset, and his traditional Navajo culture and way of life was remarkably and wonderfully redeemed.

Pete could not sing a western style song if his life depended on it, but he can sure sing in a traditional Navajo chant style. He replaced the more than two hundred medicine man chant songs with Christian songs, praising the Lord, but in the same chant style he used as a medicine man. That's contextualization of the gospel as it should be!

Pete is truly a traditional Indian person, in the purest sense of the word. He doesn't speak English, and lives as traditionally as his ancestors. His life is a perfect example of a traditional person who found freedom and deliverance through Jesus Christ, and is growing in Christ, within the cultural identity he was raised in. He has become a strong Native Christian elder, and even serves his people in the capacity of a lay pastor.

One of the highlights of my life was to be on the platform with Pete at the 1996 Atlanta Clergy Conference sponsored by Promise Keepers, when Pete was asked to pray a blessing over Promise Keepers founder, Coach Bill McCartney and the president of Promise Keepers, Randy Phillips. Many were moved to tears as this godly Native elder publicly asked the Lord's blessing on these leaders before those forty some thousand clergy in attendance.

This process needs to be allowed in all parts of culture, including the customs (practices, habits, community action, tradition); art (drawing, painting, sculpture, architecture, poetry, music and dancing); and conveniences (effects, ways and tools of a people used to accomplish work) as earlier defined.

I believe that in this process we must always understand the potential for carnality to thwart the ways of the Spirit of God. Romans 8 reminds us of the constant ongoing battle between the spirit and the flesh. There may be times when a traditional Indian Christian may do things, within his cultural comfort zone that is in opposition to biblical teaching, just like many marginal and assimilated Indian Christians, and Anglo Christians do in their own daily walk in Christ. When that happens, again, we must trust the Spirit of God to convict of sin, just as he does with us, and repentance will be called for.

In my opinion, the biggest challenge in addressing this sensitive issue lies with the church, both the denominations, mission organizations and groups working with Indian people, and Indian Christians themselves. I'm sure many of us have had to deal with thoughts like, "As a Christian, can I, or can't I, participate in a powwow? It doesn't seem all that wrong, and I feel a cultural need not being met if I don't participate, but I have always been told that it is wrong and sinful."

For those who were raised traditionally, these issues are issues that you will need to present to God, should you come to Him. His Holy Spirit will either convict you or convince you that each of the practices and ways of your life are pleasing to Him or not. When the Spirit of God convicts you of things you must be willing to lay them aside. And then present to God the things the Spirit of God convinces you of, that are pleasing in His sight, for Him to sanctify.

For me, I am a marginal person. I was not raised traditionally, nor do I feel I need to embrace all things traditional to scratch my cultural itch. I do have to present to Him, however, all the ways, thoughts, actions and deeds that I participate in and entertain in my mind, based upon my own cultural place. I too, need to set aside the things of my culture that go against the principles of the Kingdom of God, and present to Him for His sanctifying the things of my culture that are pleasing in His sight. For each of us, this is an intensely personal ongoing process as we grow in the Lord.

When we do, we will grow in our walk in Christ and find out that when we surrender to Him, He makes us fully complete, no matter who we are or what part of Indian culture we belong to.

1   Vine Deloria, Jr. *Custer Died for Your Sins* (University of Oklahoma Press) Third Printing 1989 Pages 2-3

Chapter 7

Native
America's
Three Choices

AS I HAVE COME to the last chapter of this book, I have wrestled with a variety of ways to try and wrap up all the thoughts and ideas that I have wanted to share with the audiences this book has been directed to. This book has hopefully spoken both to the Church, and to the Christian and non-Christian Native American who has a sincere desire to know their Creator.

I end this book with just as strong of a burden for my people as I had before any word was put down on paper. I want to see the Native American people who have rejected Christ and His message realize that He really does relate to us. I want them to see that the gospel is not the "Whiteman's Gospel."

I want to see the Native American Christian church grow into maturity and stability, as we take our responsibility seriously to move from the receiving end of ministry to that of participators.

I long to see the Body of Christ not be impeded by seeing a leadership that is not reflective of the rest of the Body, and I wish to see them place more trust in the emerging Native leadership that is ready, willing and able to move Native churches to more effective ministry.

I long to see local churches fulfill their mandate of being cross-cultural, not just where it is comfortable, which is usually somewhere else around the world where we can write a check and pray a prayer for the missionaries without getting really personally involved. We do need to get involved right in our own back yard as well, ministering and reaching out to those around us with a motivation that sees beyond the plight, and sees the real potential!

In an earlier chapter, I mentioned that there were three options presented to Native people during the early days of this country. Those three options were to conform to the ways of the dominant society, be removed a safe distance from the dominant society, or be wiped out.

I believe that Native Americans are still confronted with three choices, but these three choices are different from the choices of the past. Times and circumstances have changed over the years, but these three choices are choices that date back to the Old Testament. Let me share with you what I believe are those three choices facing our people today.

One of the things I have been enjoying as of late has been to study the last words of the great elders of the Bible. As we have discussed, Native Americans honor their elders, and treat them with the respect and honor they deserve.

One of the elders of the Bible was a man named Joshua. He was chosen by God to follow Moses as the leader of the Israelites from their wanderings in the wilderness into the Promised Land God had given them.

Just before Joshua died at the age of one hundred and ten years old, he assembled the Israelites, and charged them with three choices. These three choices, I believe, are the three choices that are before us today as Native Americans.

These words of Joshua are recorded for us in Joshua 24:14-15. It says,

Now fear the Lord and serve Him with all faithfulness. Throw away the gods your forefathers worshipped beyond the River and in Egypt, and serve the Lord.

> *But if serving the Lord seems undesirable to you, then choose for yourself this day whom you will serve, whether the gods your forefathers served beyond the River, or the gods of the Amorites, in whose land you are living. But as for me and my household, we will serve the Lord.*

Three choices, and those choices are clear. First, either serve the gods of your ancestors, or serve the gods in the land you are now living, or serve the Lord.

Serve The Gods Of Our Ancestors

This choice is the first choice Joshua gave to the Israelites in that wilderness experience. It is also obviously a choice that we must face as Native people. Joshua said, "If you are going to do it, do it!"

The gods of our forefathers are many, and many of them are very strong and powerful. The deeper one goes into traditional ancestral worship, the more you must be willing to sacrifice and give up, in order to increase into the deeper levels of power.

There is a price to pay for whomever or whatever we end up serving. There's no doubt about it, you are going to serve somebody.

The question I would ask Native Americans to consider, though, should they make this their choice, is this. Do we necessarily believe that just because something is "Indian," or a part of our past way of doing things, makes it automatically right? Just because my tribe apparently used to roast our captured enemies until they puckered up doesn't mean it's the right thing to do! Do we evaluate spirituality exclusively from a Native perspective, or should we see it from the context of all the communities of the world with one Creator over all, who has given us His plan through His Holy Word?

Native people need to evaluate if what they end up worshipping brings them great peace, or is the worship of the gods of our ancestors motivated by fear? Whether we want to admit it or not, many of the traditional religions of our ancestors are fear-based religions.

Also ask yourself the question about eternity, before you make this first option your choice. Does the god you choose to follow give you the assurance of life after death, in a place that can only be described as Paradise? What is the end result of worshipping the ancestral gods you will choose to worship? Where will it ultimately take you? To where will it lead?

As Joshua, the great Elder of Israel said, choose you this day whom you will serve. If you are going to serve the gods of our ancestors, then do it!

But there is a second choice. That choice is to serve the gods in the land where you are now living.

Serve The Gods In The Land Where You Are Now Living

Contrary to our belief that America is a Christian nation, is the realization that this nation is filled with many false gods, and they too are very powerful, and are today competing for the allegiance of all of America, including the Native Americans.

Often we as Native Americans tend to look at the Anglo community in America and think that they are all Christian. But that cannot be any farther from the truth. Many Anglo Americans don't want to have a thing to do with the Gospel of Jesus Christ, nor would they desire to bow a knee in honor to Him.

It is important to realize that in God's creative order, as it relates to the spiritual realm, there are only two different powers or influences in the world today. There is the Kingdom of God, and the kingdom of Satan. It is important to realize that between these two opposing forces lies no middle, neutral ground. You are either serving the Kingdom of God, or you are serving the kingdom of Satan. The influences of these two kingdoms are felt in all aspects of modern life, and there is no escaping those influences.

Many Americans who do not believe in Jesus Christ are following other gods, whether they want to admit it or not, or whether they see it or not. Believe me, in the dominant society today in America, there are false gods in the land. These gods are increasing in their following, and in their ability to bring into bondage all who would pay homage to them. America today is just as heathen as were the pagan communities in the days of the Old Testament. Nothing has changed!

One thing is certain in my mind. In our modern day society, there are no new gods, only a repeat of the gods of the Amorites, Canaanites, Perizites, etc., of the Old Testament. These false gods have worked very effectively throughout the history of the world, and Satan is not needing to dream up something new. All he needs to do, and is doing, is repeat what he has done in the past. There are gods of the Old Testament that are living, residing, and reigning in America today.

Joshua's people, the Israelites, didn't follow his admonition to serve the Lord. When they marched into the Promised Land, there were enemies that they were to defeat, so they could possess the land. They were to drive out the inhabitants, and not serve their gods.

But they failed in their mission, even though God had promised them sure victory if they would only stay true to Him.

In fact, we read of their failure in the next book of the Old Testament, the book of Judges. In Judges 3:7, we read,

> *The Israelites did evil in the eyes of the Lord; they forgot the Lord their God and served the Baals and the Asherahs.*

Who were the "Baals and the Asherahs" of the Old Testament?

Baal was a Babylonian deity, who was often referred to as "Lord, or Sun God." In the Old Testament there are more than one hundred and twenty references to this idol. He was believed to give fertility to the womb, and life giving rain to the soil. The worship of Baal involved sacred prostitution and even child sacrifice, as Jeremiah 19:5 says.

> *They have built the high places of Baal to burn their sons in the fire as offerings to Baal—something I did not command or mention, nor did it enter my mind.*

Asherah was another deity, a female Babylonian goddess who was considered to be the wife of Baal. She was considered to be the beautiful goddess of war and fertility. She was known as Ishtar in Babylonia and Athtart in Aram. The Greeks called her Astarte or Aphrodite, while the Romans referred to her as Venus.

Canaanite worship was sold out to the Baals and the Asherahs. The Israelites forsook their God and began to worship these false gods after they had entered into the Promised Land.

Worship of Asherah in the Old Testament was associated with all forms of sexual immorality and extreme lascivious practices. Her priests were eunuchs, dressed as women. Her female devotees were temple prostitutes, and her male followers were involved in all forms of sexual orgies.

How do you worship in the tradition of Asherah? Worship of Asherah always centered around the reproductive organs of the human anatomy. The worshipers of these deities inevitably got bored with normal sexual relations, and became desirous of more and more deviant forms of sex to satisfy their sexual cravings. They were never satisfied until their appetite for flesh finally got what it wanted, that being human sacrifice.

When they worshipped, nudity was involved, and wild sexual cravings were unleashed, until the lowest, most blatant forms of sexual behavior were reached, including bestiality (sex with animals), sodomy, incest, rape, and orgies.

My friend, do you realize that the Baals and Asherahs have moved from Canaan to North America? They are here. The streets of our cities are filled with temples to the goddess Asherah. Adult book stores, peep shows, massage parlors and the like are all establishments where worship of the reproductive parts of the human anatomy is promoted. But now it is not just avenues outside our homes where such activities are promoted.

That which would have been considered deviant and reprehensive behavior in our country in the past, causing great shame and embarrassment to those involved, is now the ticket to appear on the various T.V. talk shows shown across the U.S. and Canada..

Homosexuals, lesbians, transvestites, transsexuals, cross-dressers and the like are parading their wares in home after home through these talk shows where there are seemingly no boundaries. The more deviant the topic, the higher the ratings seem to be.

These are now considered normal forms of behavior in our

country, while those who would stand for biblical, and might I add, even Native American traditional values are now considered far right militants and extremists.

We now live in a land where wrong has become right, right has become wrong, and every man does what seems to be right in his own eyes, based upon the situations he finds himself in. We no longer are led by a code of moral ethics that are either biblical or even Native traditional, for those don't seem to apply to this "enlightened modern society."

Asherah worship is running rampant across our country, and can be accessed in new and powerful ways that were never available to this country even ten years ago.

In the past, if a person would desire sexual services outside the bonds of marriage, that person would have to leave his home and travel to the seedy side of a city, or the "red light district," to engage in Asherah worship. Not anymore. Through the advanced technology of cable television, the video rental industry, direct broadcasting services, pay-per-view television, and even the computer Internet, the goddess Asherah is now able to visit the majority of homes in North America as never before. You can sit in the comfort of your easy chair, right in your own home, and engage in the worship of Asherah as you focus in on the reproductive parts of the human anatomy of those parading before you on the screen.

The sanctity and protective haven of the home has been dismantled in America, and now even our homes are not protected from the evil of the gods in the land we are now living.

Even with pornography being "scrambled" by the cable industry, the sound is usually projected unhindered, and even scrambled stations can be easily watched, with literally millions of Americans engaging in and becoming addicted to such practices.

Many Native Americans are being caught up in addictions to pornography and its impact is even spreading across Native country like a plague.

Let me share with you a paper I wrote for the Religious Alli-

ance Against Pornography (RAAP) in 1995, on the growing problem pornography is having in our Native communities, to illustrate just how awful this problem is among our people:

The Problem of Pornography in Native America

At one time, the evil of pornography was once not thought
to be a problem extending into Native homes and communities.
But it has now become another tool in the destruction of the
Native culture and family structure.

Much of the traditional and ancestral culture of Native
America has been lost over the years, but a look back historically
shows that most Native cultures in North America treated women
with respect and honor, with some cultures even being matriar-
chal. Children have always had a special place in traditional tribal
systems, and to abuse or exploit them would have been unthink-
able and intolerable.

The growing problem of pornography, and all the other vices
it promotes, runs against the traditional values and culture of
our people, and its growing influence must be stopped.

In Native communities across North America, access to pornography has escalated in proportion to the rest of the North
American population. It used to be that the availability of pornography was isolated from Native communities, and found only
in the cities through adult bookstores and other pornography
outlets. One would have had to leave their community and venture many miles to access pornography, but times have changed.

The changing culture of our Native American population has
been a contributing factor to the growing problem of pornography, and all the other vices it fuels.

Since 1786, the U.S. government has successively adopted the
policies of assimilation, removal, allotment, reservations, local
communities, relocation, and finally self-determination. One of
the more influential acts of the government in the 1950's, as it
relates to pornography, was the Indian Relocation Act. This act
removed a vast number of Native Americans from their reservations to the cities of America. Many Native people suffered
culture shock in this move and returned back to their reserva-

tions. Many others survived and became urbanized. Subsequent generations have been raised in urban life, removing them further and further from their roots.

The end result of the urban migration of the past 40 years is illustrated by a study of the 1990 census. According to that census, more than one half of Native Americans now live in urbanized centers, most of which live in the lower socio-economic class, and consequently in the poverty centers of our cities. As we know, it is in just such parts of cities where pornography, prostitution, and other sex industries are found.

Urban Indians have become desensitized to the corruption around them, and find themselves unable, for the most part, to move upward and outward from such surroundings. Some urbanized Indians have decided to move back to the reservations, while others frequently visit "back home," as a part of the extended family network common to Indian culture.

All too often, the urbanized people who return permanently or periodically to the reservation, brings with them their own form of culture, which has been exposed to the "white man's world," and all the vice it entails.

The end result is the propagation of activities such as introducing pornography to extended family and friends back home, abuse of extended family members, and all other forms of sexual sins which pornography fuels.

For those who remained on the reservation, access to pornographic materials has become more readily available, especially in the last decade. This is due primarily to the accessibility of satellite television and the video cassette rental industry.

Most reservations today have numerous video rental facilities, and the rentals offered range from G to XXX rated merchandise.

Because of the isolation factor on many reservations, cable television services are only now becoming available, but limited in scope to urban communities. Rural dwellers only access to the outside world has been limited to satellite reception, and its growth and usage cannot be understated.

In my numerous visits to reservations nationwide, I have been amazed at the number of satellite dishes dotting the Indian landscape. I recall visiting on the Turtle Mountain Reservation in northern North Dakota about ten years ago, and in one development of about thirty government homes, it seemed like every back yard had a satellite receiver! On a visit to an isolated part of the Navajo reservation, I was amazed to pass by a traditional Navajo hogan (traditional home made of cedar logs and mud) and a satellite dish mounted next to the sheep corral. This area was not even serviced by electricity.

As I visited in that hogan, I found that after the sun went down, the family would put their sheep back in their corral. They then would start up a generator and spend hours watching their big screen television as they sat on sheepskin rugs on the dirt floor. Because they were very traditional, and their access to the outside world was minimal, the television became their window to the world. Everything and anything would be watched, all the way from sports to soaps to movies and pornography.

In the late 1970s, the Canadian government provided satellite receivers and transmitters to many isolated Native community across the north country of Canada. Indian and Inuit villages that were very traditional because of their isolation, were now introduced to the outside world of violence, materialism, and pornography. All of the programming available by satellite was accessed, and was, in an unregulated form, broadcast to every home in these villages.

In an article published by the *Winnipeg Free Press*, several years after this program was underway, it reported some amazing findings. It stated that once cohesive and united villages, living in much the same way they had lived for generations, were undergoing massive changes.

Crime became rampant, incidents of child and spousal abuse rose sharply, and according to the report, the government could not build reformatories and detention facilities fast enough to cope with the number of criminals, especially youth, that were being prosecuted.

Interrelated Problems

Within Native America, the problem of pornography must be viewed in the context of our culture, and as one of many interrelated problems. Alcoholism, unemployment and hopelessness, along with pornography, interrelate and provide fuel for each other.

The particular aspect of Native culture that must be considered as interrelated with the problem of pornography is the emphasis on the extended family unit.

Because of this emphasis, most Native homes extend beyond the nuclear family to include other relatives, even distant ones, as a normal part of the household. As previously mentioned, the mobility of urbanized Indians who often return to the reservation brings many extended family members back into reservation homes.

All too often extended relatives who are in Native homes are the ones who end up introducing the children and youth in the home to pornography brought back from the cities. They also are the ones who engage in the abuse and molestation of the children and youth of that home. This, in my counseling experience, seems to be a normal and frequent occurrence in Native homes nationwide.

Common law situations, broken relationships and failed marriages abound on reservations. When marriages and relationships fail, often those affected by it move in with other family. They bring into the home not only their physical presence but their grief, heartbreak and despair. If they have been into pornography, the fuel for abuse of especially children and youth of the home they are in is obvious. It is a sad commentary, but the reality is that if you grow up in a Native home today, to be abused and molested is more than likely the norm, rather than the exception.

According to one contemporary Indian writer, the problem of alcoholism affects close to 80% of the Indian population nationwide. The curse of alcoholism is directly interrelated with the problem of pornography. It is a known fact that alcoholism desensitizes a person and they become more free to say things, and do things that they normally would not do in a sober state.

Alcohol abuse, spousal and child abuse, and molestation goes hand in hand. The conclusion can be drawn that when a Native person is exposed to pornographic materials, and then alcohol is introduced into the equation, the end result is a person who is more willing to carry out the fantasies in their mind, and put thought into action.

At first glance, unemployment would not seem to be a contributing factor to the problem of pornography. But once again, this definitely is a major contributing factor to a growing addiction to pornography across Indian America.

On all too many reservations, unemployment is not just a minor problem, but rampant. There are some reservations that up until recently, had unemployment rates of up to 90 percent. Many reservations had unemployment rates well above 50 percent, while the majority had rates well over the national average.

This problem is being solved, so to speak, on many reservations with the growth of the gambling and gaming industry. There are some reservations now that have a job for every person who wants to work, and they are all provided through the casinos and gambling facilities springing up across Indian America.

Though it is solving the job crisis on many reservations, the gambling industry is bringing into many communities new and powerful addictions. Organized crime is reported to be involved in some reservation gaming programs, and their ties to pornography and prostitution cannot be disputed. Only time will tell of what adverse impact this industry will have in Native communities nationwide.

When you don't have a job, however, one thing is evident. You end up with a lot of time on your hands. I heard recently that when the cable television industry was beginning, the largest blocs of subscribers were those who were unemployed and living below the poverty level. The rationale for that was obvious. If you have a large portion of time on your hands, with nothing to do, entertainment becomes the means to fill the void.

Across Indian America, there still are many who have time on their hands, and so they fill their time with items of amusement. The viewing of entertaining videos, movies, etc., available through cable television, pay per view, satellite, direct broadcasting services (DBS), and other such vehicles for pornography are what many Native Americans have become addicted to.

The growing pressure of this assault is being felt in all ages, but in particular among the many Native youth. They are being hit from two fronts today. The first being the pressure to return to the traditional worship and ways of ancestors. The second is from the paganistic front of the dominant society through music, MTV, videos, video games, the information superhighway, etc. Unfortunately, most Indian young people have been ill equipped to deal with these strong and powerful challenges.

The effects of these challenges on our youth are already being felt today. Of great concern will be the long term effects on that generation in the years to follow. What was said of the Israelites after their entrance into the Promised Land just might end up being the descriptive term for this generation of Indian youth.

After that whole generation had been gathered to their fathers, another generation grew up, who knew neither the Lord nor what He had done for Israel. Judges 2:10

The youth are not the only ones being affected today. The fact that all too many Native adults have too much time on their hands, and consequently fill that time with Hollywood garbage, and then abuse alcohol, often in an extended family environment, is a blending of obviously damaging elements, that lead all too often to abuse and molestation of the worst sort.

The growing availability of pornographic materials through satellite, videos, pay per view, DBS, and even the information superhighway all point to one sobering truth. Unless we begin the process of confronting this evil, we will see an increase in the cultural destruction of the Native American people.

Pornography is not an isolated problem, either in content or in access. It is a part of a larger problem, with many interrelated parts, all of which are damaging alone, but when combined together, provide one of the major fronts of spiritual, emotional and even physical destruction of a people who cannot afford to lose any more of their identity or populace.[1]

There are two other false gods listed in the Old Testament that are often mentioned with Baal and Asherah. Those gods are named "Molech" and "Chemosh." Molech was the national pagan god of the Ammonites and Chemosh was the national pagan god of the Moabites. Worship of both of these pagan gods involved the sacrificing of innocent children.

Who were the Ammonites and the Moabites? Scripture tells us that they are the offspring of Lot and his two daughters, after they fled from the destruction in Sodom and Gomorrah. In Genesis 19 we read of the climate of Sodom and Gomorrah during the days Lot lived there. The area was steeped deeply in homosexual sin, and because of the wickedness there, God was intent on destroying it. As Lot and his family fled the area, we see that his wife looked back, and God turned her into a pillar of salt. Lot and his two daughters were reduced to living in the caves, and it was there that his daughters conspired to get their father drunk and sleep with him so they could preserve their family line. That happened, and both daughters conceived. The oldest daughter gave birth to a son whom she named Moab, and the youngest daughter gave birth to a son, and she named him Ben-Ammi. Moab's descendants became the Moabites, who served Chemosh, while Ben-Ammi's descendants became the Ammonites, who worshipped the detestable god Molech.

From a culture that welcomed, embraced and promoted homosexuality to the incestuous relationship of Lot and his daughters came the peoples who degenerated so low as to offer helpless and innocent children as sacrifices to their national pagan gods.

Molech was a huge, hollow metal god, and this idol was formed with his hands extended. The followers of Molech would build a fire in the hollowed out portion of this metal idol. When Molech burned bright red from the intensity of the fire within, the worship of this idol would begin.

People would bring their children up to this fiery hot idol, and place their children in the arms of Molech, and then watch as their children literally burned to death, as a sacrifice to this god.

The progression always has been from Baal, to Asherah, to Molech and Chemosh.

In fact, Scripture minces no words when it comes to describing these detestable forms of worship of these false, pagan gods.

We read in Psalms 106:34-38:

They did not destroy the peoples as the Lord had commanded them, but they mingled with the nations and adopted their customs. They worshipped their idols, which became a snare to them. They sacrificed their sons and their daughters to demons. They shed innocent blood, the blood of their sons and daughters, whom they sacrificed to the idols of Canaan, and the land was desecrated by their blood.

Molech and Chemosh have also moved from the Old Testament, and they too, have taken up residence in North America today, and are being worshipped right along side the Baals and the Asherahs.

My involvement in the Religious Alliance Against Pornography has been one of the most difficult responsibilities I have ever had to shoulder, because of the information that we receive on just how bad our country and the rest of the world has become as it relates to these gods.

Children often are the victims of the pornography industry, in sickening and reprehensible productions. Some are even being murdered by their sexual predators, while the cameras are rolling!

You can actually access through the underground these video tapes, and watch innocent children not only being sexually abused, but even murdered, all for the sexual pleasure and fulfillment of deviant adults!

Sexual deviancy always leads to the ultimate craving for flesh, human sacrifice. Men who are hooked on pornography are much more likely to commit rape, incest and other sexually related crimes, according to the statistics. Women who are becoming pregnant because of casual sex outside of the bonds of marriage are sacrificing many of the children that are still in their wombs to the burning arms of Molech through abortion. Millions of unborn babies are sacrificed to Molech each year in America, all because of the sexual cravings and subsequent deviant behavior of men and women across our land.

The futures of many children are altered for life because they have suffered at the hands of even their fathers or other family members through incest, and molestation, and it happens all too often in our Native communities!

The pain and hurt that many Native people have suffered from because of the worship of these gods goes on and on and on. In a very real sense, any victim of sexual abuse has been offered as a sacrifice into the burning arms of Molech because of the sins of their predators.

Pay-per-view television has brought the sex industry right into our homes, along with the video rental industry, and now one of the biggest challenges we face is with computer cyberporn.

Through the Internet and the World Wide Web, any and all kinds of deviant pornographic materials can be accessed, and at this time, we have little control over who can get a hold of this information, including our own children.

Our children are much more computer literate than we as parents are, and any child, no matter how old they are, can access in less than three and one half minutes, the most disgusting and reprehensible forms of pornography, and we as their parents wouldn't even know it!

I was amazed at some of the statistics shared with us by Dr. Jerry Kirk, co-chairman of the Religious Alliance Against Pornography.

He shared that of all the items and services available through the World Wide Web, only about 10 to 11 percent is what is referred to as "news rooms." This is where you can go in and dialogue with people, world wide on a variety of subjects, and access information, data, photos, etc., on a wide variety of common interests.

Of that 10 - 11 percent of materials available from news rooms, only about 3.5 percent of the 10 percent is pornographic in nature. So really pornography makes up a very small percentage of available material on the Internet. But listen to this.

Of all the downloads available through all of the Internet, more than 85 percent are pornographic in nature.

Yes, Baal, Asherah, Chemosh and Molech have arrived and are some of the immigrants who have joined the rest of the world here in America. Many are being caught up in their pagan forms of worship, and it is spreading like wild fire across our land.

Baal, Asherah and Molech are only a few of the many gods that are in the land that we are now living in. We haven't even discussed other gods, such as the gods of materialism, pleasure and violence.

We have the option, Joshua says, to serve the gods in the land you are now living, but oh, it comes at such a price.

But thank God there's a third option, and one that I would plead with you today to choose. That third option, Joshua says is this, "but as for me and my household, we will serve the Lord."

Serve The Lord

In reality, my friend, there really is no other option!

In a very real sense, the soul of the Native American people is under attack from many strong and powerful fronts. The eternal destiny of our people hangs in the balance, and if we are to be saved eternally, it will come not from our ancestral ways, it will come not from our embracing the gods in the land we are now living, but will come only when we surrender our lives to the one the Bible says is the Way, the Truth and the Life. For you see, no man or woman, no matter what tribe around this globe he or she may be from, can come to the Father, the Creator of heaven and earth, except by Jesus Christ. He is our only hope.

What does it mean, then, to come to Christ?

We need to see that the message of the Bible is God reaching down to man, not man reaching up to God.

All the religions of the world are man's attempts, within his own culture and ways, to reach out and attempt to appease God, based on his assumptions about God.

God has revealed Himself to the world, and He has done that through the writings of Holy Scripture.

He has established a plan that is His, not man's, for the redemption of the world back to Himself. When we follow that plan, we will be assured that He will accept us, forgive us, cleanse us, and redeem us to Himself.

In a very real sense, Christianity is not a religion, it is a relationship. A relationship with our Creator that is based not on fear, but on peace, on righteousness, not on wickedness, on hope, and not on hopelessness.

To be made right with God, you need to come to Him, just as you are, with all the baggage of sin, and accept His free gift of forgiveness, which he provided for us when He died on the Cross.

Being reconciled with God involves accepting Christ's sacrifice of His life on the cross as the penalty for your sins. Do not seek any other form of sacrifice for your sins, because God has provided the spotless, sinless and perfect sacrificial Lamb, when He allowed His only Son, Jesus, to die on the cross.

As we accept Christ's substitutionary penalty for our sins, we also need to repent of our sins to God. In the Old Testament, the root word for repent was a Hebrew word that meant "to sigh or breath deeply." As a parent of three children, I know what this means.

My kids love ice cream, and when they were young, they could spot a Dairy Queen store miles away.

"Dad, we want ice cream!" they would shout as we drove along the street approaching this temptation. They would increase in volume and excitement the closer we got to the store. I would be firm in my saying no, usually because my wallet wasn't in the best of shape, but that would not deter them.

Finally, as we got close to the driveway into the ice cream shop, I would finally give in, breathing a big sigh, and say, "OK, you win, let's get some ice cream!"

The deep sigh preceded the change in mind that provided my children with their ice cream. That's what repentance really means.

Repentance is getting to a point when you have been going in one direction for so long, and you finally reach a point of changing your mind, changing your direction, and changing your life. That deep sigh we often give when we change our mind about an incessant plea of a child for ice cream is the same mentality we must have if we are to repent of our sins. It represents a complete and total surrender of our ways to the one who is our Creator, and the giver of our lives.

When we repent, and accept Christ, Scripture says that Christ forgives, and accepts us into his family. We then become heirs of all that is His, including the blessing of His presence in our life now, and the hope that we will be with Him in paradise throughout all eternity.

Once we accept Christ as our Savior that begins the process of pursuing God for the remainder of our lives. The pursuit of God is an ongoing journey, and one that provide us with the most wonderful and fulfilling life here on earth.

The Bible says in Jeremiah 29:13 that, *"You will seek me and find me when you seek me with all your heart."*

Christianity is not just an experience of accepting Christ, and that's it. It is an ongoing process of developing an intimate relationship with our Creator, and in being with Him, we desire nothing else on earth.

There is a deep powerful level of existence available to the believer that, unfortunately, not many Christians have found. There are many Christians who have focused solely on the accepting Christ part of salvation, and have not desired any further cravings of God since their conversion. That is why many Christians today don't act any different, look any different, or think any differently from those unbelievers around them. They are living in a shallow experience, carnal in thinking, and not able to be victorious over the habits of the past. Unfortunately, Native Americans have met so many Christians who live at this surface level of Christianity, and that makes following Christ so unappealing.

But believe me, there truly is a deeper life for any person, which begins when they accept Christ, and continues to develop throughout the rest of their life. This level is not easily explained in human words, but is wonderfully expressed by the divinely inspired words of the psalmist in the 42nd Psalm:

As the deer pants for streams of water, so my soul pants for you, O God. My soul thirsts for God, for the Living God. When can I go and meet with God?

When we reach this level of pursuing God, an indescribable experience with Him awaits us as described in Psalms 73:21-26:

I am always with you; you hold me by your right hand. You guide me with your counsel and afterwards you will take me into glory. Whom have I in heaven but you? And earth has nothing I desire besides you. My flesh and my heart may fail, but God is the strength of my heart, and my portion forever.

True victorious Christian living is, at its best, an ever deepening of our relationship with our Creator. Salvation enables us to deal with the past, and be reconciled to our Creator, and from that moment on, we begin a journey with Him that no man has ever completed, for with the Lord, there is neither limit nor end.

God is a Person, and in the depth of His nature, He desires to be known, just as we desire to be known. He longs to be loved, just as we long to be loved. He desires to develop a relationship with us, just like we long to develop relationships and friendships with others. Developing a relationship with God truly is like developing a relationship with others.

The basic principles apply in human relationships and in heavenly relationships.

After over a quarter century of traveling and ministering in many communities, I can say that I have met a vast number of people. But this vast number of people I know only from a distance. My communication with these people is in very general terms, and I don't reveal much of myself to these people, because they are just acquaintances.

There are a smaller number of people, taken from this large

group of acquaintances, who I know better. My colleagues in ministry are an example of this level of relationships. I know them by name, and share many similarities with them. We can talk at a deeper level, because I know them more personally than just casual acquaintances.

But then the circle gets smaller, and there would be a few that I would say are real "good friends." At this level of friendship, we talk more intimately. We know what each other's children are doing, and do things together that we wouldn't do with the larger body of acquaintances.

Then, down at a very deep level, are only one or two very close, intimate friendships.

God gave to me a friend at this level, only several years ago. We share a friendship on a level that is deeper than any other level of friendship I know, outside of my marriage. We talk on a level that is very open and intimate, and we can say things to each other from our hearts, and that is an amazing thing. Our friendship will last for a lifetime, and for that I am grateful.

Then there is one other level of friendship and relationship that is as deep as is humanly possible. That is the relationship that I have with my wife. She knows me like no other, and the level of communication we share together is as deep as one can go. We have become, as the Bible says, "One Flesh." There truly is a mystery of two people, joining together in marriage, becoming "one." What a joy it is to share that most intimate level of friendship and relationship created beings can enjoy.

The basic difference between my relationship with my wife and that of casual acquaintances is the amount of time we have spent together. When we fell in love, all we wanted to do was be together, and get to know one another more. The more time we spent together, the more we knew each other, and could demonstrate a deeper and deeper love and commitment to each other.

So it is with our relationship with our Creator, in the framework of Christian faith. Once I accept Christ, I then begin a process of spending time with my Creator, developing a relationship with Him through His Word. I move from a relationship of a casual acquaintance, to the deepest level of intimacy mankind is allowed to have, reserved for the Creator and His creation. That's true Christianity, and Christianity that is available   to Native Americans, when we choose the third option, to serve the Lord.

Let me close this book with, what is to me, one of the most encouraging words from the Bible, especially for us as Native Americans. It relates to the relationship just described above, and is illustrated for us in the Old Testament. We as Native people can find so many similarities to our way of life in it.

When the Lord allowed the Israelites to go into the Promised Land, He divided up among the tribes allotments of land. All twelve tribes, except one, received portions of this land that flowed with milk and honey.

The one tribe that did not receive any allotment of land was the Levite tribe. God said to the Levites simply, in Deuteronomy 18:1-2:

The priests, who are Levites—indeed the whole tribe of Levi—are to have no allotment or inheritance with Israel. They shall live on the offerings made to the Lord by fire, for that is their inheritance. They shall have no inheritance among their brothers; the Lord is their inheritance, as he promised them.

By those very words, God made the Levites richer than all his brothers, richer than all the kings and rulers who have ever lived in this world.

For you see, the man who has God for his treasure has more than anyone in the world. He may not have many earthly belongings, or perhaps, like our people, had so much of our land, languages and identities taken away from us. As painful as that was, and is, if our people would come to Christ, I honestly believe that God, knowing our struggles in the past, would bless Native America with so much more than all the land we used to possess, our lives would be even more full than any Native person has ever experienced, either before or after so much of our identity, lands and languages were taken from us.

When we have God as our Savior, all human things are not

necessary to our happiness and fulfillment. Or, as we have had to see them go, acre by acre, language by language, identity by identity, we will scarcely feel a sense of loss, for having God, the Creator of all things, we have more than any earthly possession affords.

The options are clear for us today in Native America. The question that must be answered by all who are concerned about the incredible challenge facing the Body of Christ, as it approaches Native America, is "what will we do to meet this need?"

Will Native churches take their responsibility seriously to continue to push for the needed changes that will allow the gospel to penetrate our culture, and develop truly biblically based churches that are outwardly focused?

Will denominational leadership be willing to evaluate their methodologies and assumptions used in reaching Native Americans? Will we have the boldness to repent of the past, reevaluate for the present, and retool for the future?

And finally, will the Native American community be willing to put aside misconceptions about the gospel of Jesus Christ that are not based on the facts, and finally give consideration to the message of the gospel, regardless of the past methods that were wrong and shrouded the truth from us?

If all three communities were willing to move from their entrenched positions that have been in place for centuries, it would be for the betterment of Native America, and for that matter, the whole world!

Lord, may it be so!

1   Craig S. Smith, *The Problem of Pornography in Native America, To the Religious Alliance Against Pornography* (RAAP), 1995

Jesus, the Creator's Son

JESUS WAS GOD with a body, a Jew in Galilee with a family, a person who in a way was just like everyone else. Yet he was different than anyone who had ever lived on earth before.

He is born as a member of the Tribe of Judah, as part of a minority people group living under the Roman colonizers. The dominant language and culture of his day is Greek.

He grows up the object of shame from family and neighbours that Joseph was not his real dad.

Politics determined where he would spend his growing up years in Egypt as a refugee infant, and Nazareth which is under the control of Herod, whom Jesus later refers to as a fox.

He grows up during a period of revived Jewish identity and pride. Jews were commonly regarded as social misfits because of their customs and were the object of racist jokes. As an adult he respects and observes many of the customs of his people.

His ministry is very relational. He is very approachable. He wants people to know this, and they do. Contrary to most of the Bible teachers of his day, He meets people where they are at.

He is very perceptive. He has an amazing ability to see beneath peoples' layers and know what they long for, or what they really believe, but are afraid of revealing.

He is not afraid to provoke people. Wherever he goes, he produces a crisis. He is always compelling people to decide, to make a choice.

After living a perfect life (He is GOD!), he becomes the ultimate victim as he is unjustly nailed to a cross for sins he's never committed. At the same time, he lays down his life willingly to pay the ultimate sacrifice for the sin and shame of the whole world. He fulfills the just demands of a holy God. His hands will always carry the scars. He's so poor he is buried in a borrowed grave.

Three days later he walks out of that grave, proving his power even over death.

—Dan Woodard

Do you know
the
Creator's Son?

PERHAPS YOU HAVE always thought that Christianity was *The Whiteman's Gospel.* Because of this, you have kept away from anything to do with the Bible or Jesus Christ.

After reading *Whiteman's Gospel,* do you feel that Jesus truly is the Creator God's Son? Is He speaking to you? Would you like to respond to what you have just read about believing in Jesus?

Here are five things you need to know to believe in Jesus as your Savior:

You need to—

REPENT—Be sorry for the wrong things you have done—sorry enough to quit them. "God did not remember these times when people did not know better. But now He tells all men everywhere to be sorry for their sins and to turn from them." Acts 17:30

CONFESS—Tell God you have sinned. "If you say with your mouth that Jesus is Lord, and believe in your heart that God raised Him from the dead, you will be saved from the punishment of sin." Romans 10:9

BELIEVE— Jesus died for you. "Put your trust in the Lord Jesus Christ and you...will be saved from the punishment of sin." Acts 16:31

ASK —God to forgive you. "If we tell Him our sins, He is faithful and we can depend on Him to forgive us our sins. He will make our lives clean from all sin." 1 John 1:9

RECEIVE—Jesus as your Savior. "he gave the right and the power to become children of God, to those who receive Him...to those who put their trust in His Name." John 1:12

If you want to ask Jesus Christ into your life, pray the following pray or say in your own words what is printed below:

> *Dear Jesus, I realize I am a sinner. I long for peace in my heart. I believe you are the Holy Son of God, that you came down and died on the cross for my sins. Thank you for doing this for me. I am sorry for my sins. Please forgive me. With your help, I will turn my back on them. By faith, I receive you into my life as my personal Savior and Lord. From now on, I want to please you.*

If you have followed these steps and asked Christ to take control of your life, get a copy of God's Word, the Bible, and begin reading it. Also start talking to God in prayer. Go to church regularly. Choose a church where God's message of salvation is taught.

If you have prayed the above prayer, the publishers of "Whiteman's Gospel" would like to hear from you. Please write your name on the coupon below, or if you don't want up cut up this book, just write on another sheet of paper, and mail it to:

Indian Life Books
P.O. Box 3765, RPO Redwood Centre
Winnipeg, MB Canada R2W 3R6

— — — — — — — — — — — — — — — — — — —

I prayed the prayer suggested in "Whiteman's Gospel" and now I would like more information on how to live as a Christian.

Please write to me and tell me the name of someone who can give me personal help.

Name _____

Address _____

Town _____

State/Prov _____ Zip/Postal_____